NICKELODEON

降击神

AVATAR

THE LAST AIRBENDER™

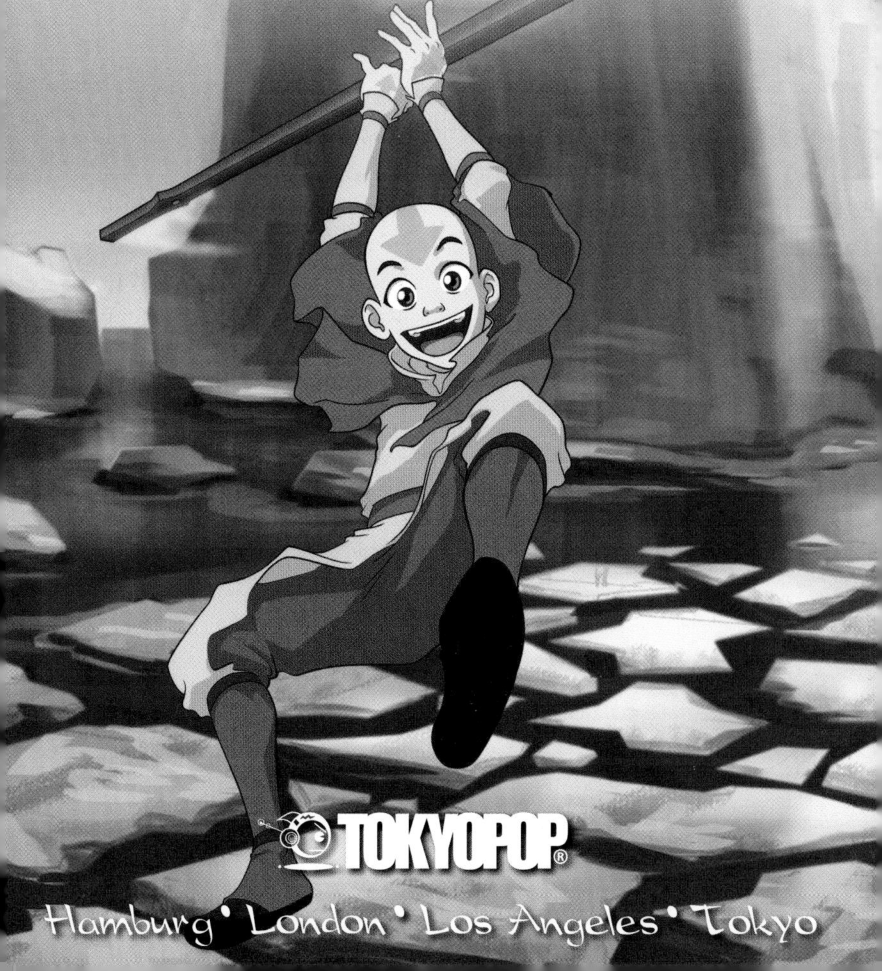

TOKYOPOP®

Hamburg • London • Los Angeles • Tokyo

Editor - Zachary Rau
Contributing Editor - Robert Langhorn
Graphic Designer, Letterer & Cover Designer - Tomás Montalvo-Lagos
Graphic Artists - Anna Kernbaum, John Lo and Monalisa J. de Asis

Digital Imaging Manager - Chris Buford
Production Managers - Jennifer Miller and Mutsumi Miyazaki
Senior Designer - Anna Kernbaum
Senior Editor - Elizabeth Hurchalla
Managing Editor - Lindsey Johnston
VP of Production - Ron Klamert
Publisher & Editor in Chief - Mike Kiley
President & C.O.O. - John Parker
C.E.O. - Stuart Levy

E-mail: info@TOKYOPOP.com
Come visit us online at www.TOKYOPOP.com

A **TOKYOPOP** Cine-Manga® Book
TOKYOPOP Inc.
5900 Wilshire Blvd., Suite 2000
Los Angeles, CA 90036

Avatar: The Last Airbender Chapter 2

ISBN: 1-59532-892-0

First TOKYOPOP® printing: May 2006

10 9 8 7 6 5 4 3 2

Printed in the USA

NICKELODEON

降世神通

AVATAR

THE LAST AIRBENDER

Created By

Michael Dante DiMartino &

Bryan Konietzko

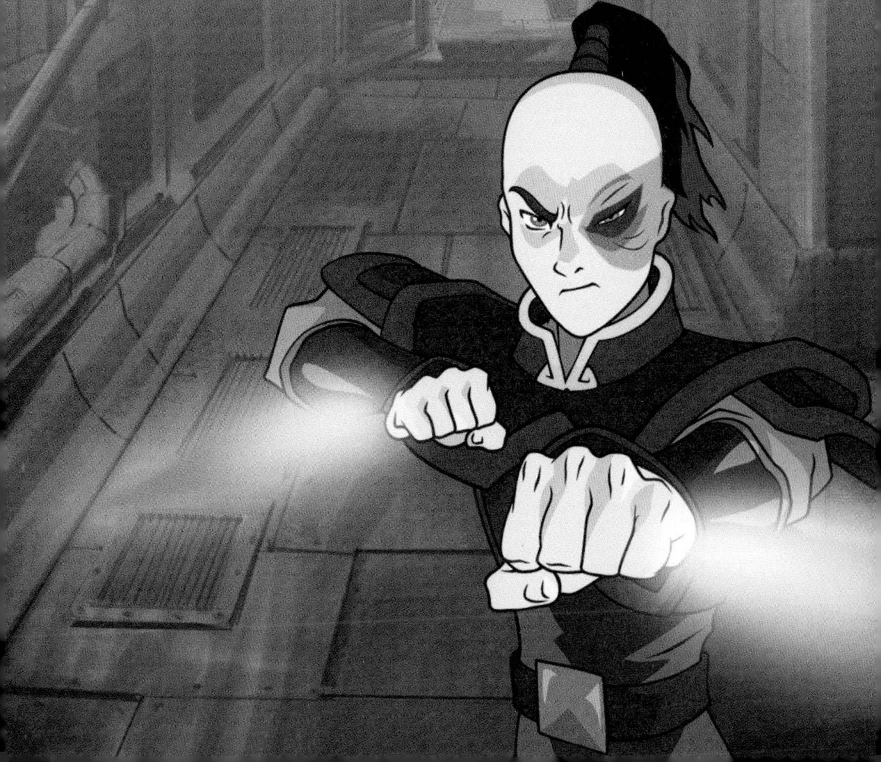

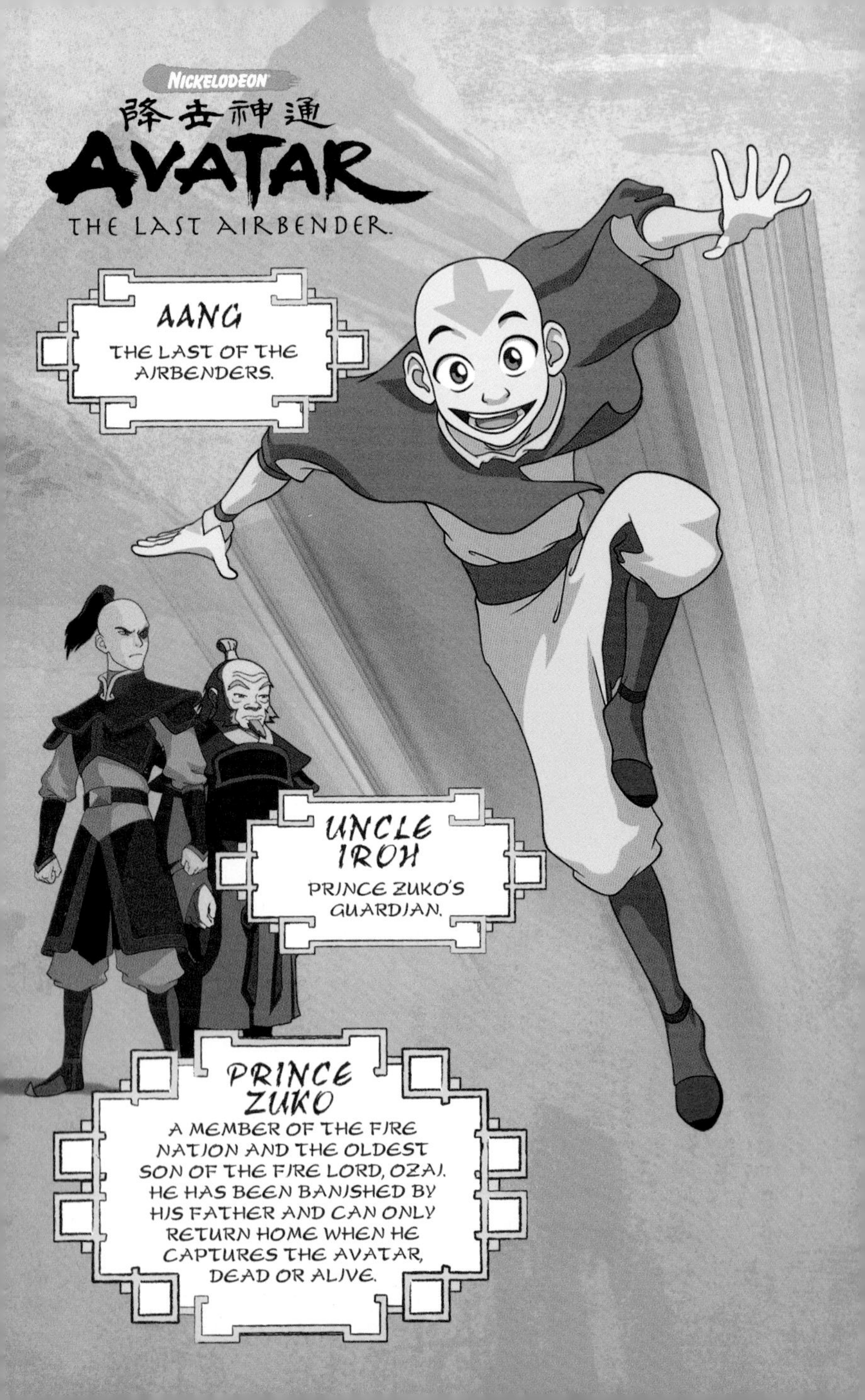
NICKELODEON
降去神通
AVATAR
THE LAST AIRBENDER.
AANG
THE LAST OF THE AIRBENDERS.
UNCLE IROH
PRINCE ZUKO'S GUARDIAN.
PRINCE ZUKO
A MEMBER OF THE FIRE NATION AND THE OLDEST SON OF THE FIRE LORD, OZAI. HE HAS BEEN BANISHED BY HIS FATHER AND CAN ONLY RETURN HOME WHEN HE CAPTURES THE AVATAR, DEAD OR ALIVE.

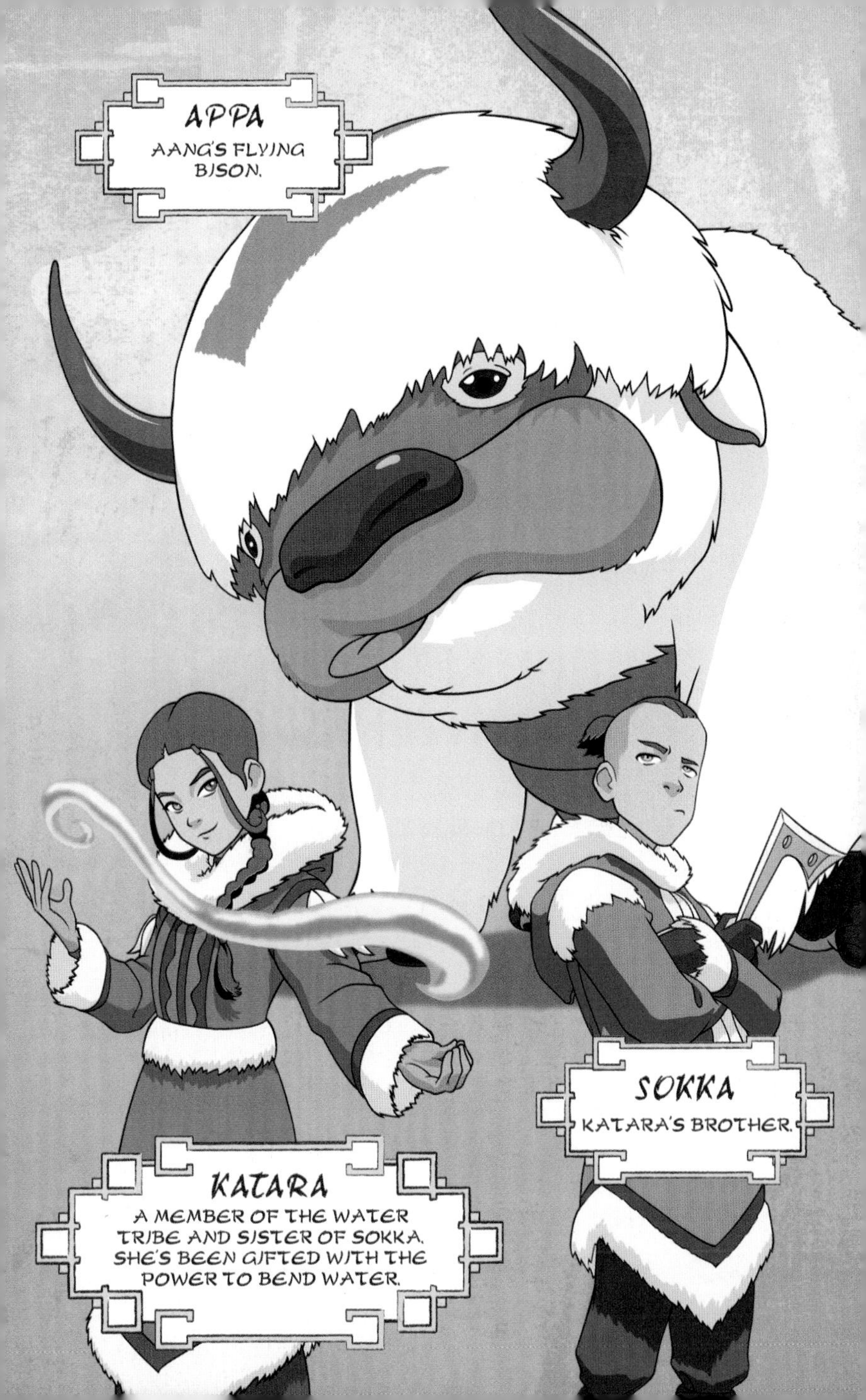
APPA
AANG'S FLYING BISON.
SOKKA
KATARA'S BROTHER.
KATARA
A MEMBER OF THE WATER TRIBE AND SISTER OF SOKKA. SHE'S BEEN GIFTED WITH THE POWER TO BEND WATER.

NICKELODEON

AVATAR
THE LAST AIRBENDER

CHAPTER 2:
CONTENTS

THE STORY SO FAR...

WHILE OUT FISHING, KATARA AND HER BROTHER SOKKA DISCOVER A YOUNG BOY CALLED AANG AND HIS FLYING BISON, APPA, TRAPPED IN AN ICEBERG. BREAKING HIM OUT OF HIS FROZEN PRISON, THEY LEARN THAT HE IS AN AIRBENDER AND HAS BEEN TRAPPED IN THE ICE FOR A HUNDRED YEARS.

THE GROUP RETURNS TO THE WATER TRIBE'S VILLAGE, NOT KNOWING THAT FREEING AANG HAS ALERTED A FIRE NAVY WARSHIP CARRYING THE TERRIBLE PRINCE ZUKO.

NOW PRINCE ZUKO KNOWS THE SECRET LOCATION OF THE WATER VILLAGE AND IS ON HIS WAY TO DESTROY IT. WILL SOKKA, KATARA AND AANG FIND OUT IN TIME TO SAVE THE VILLAGE?

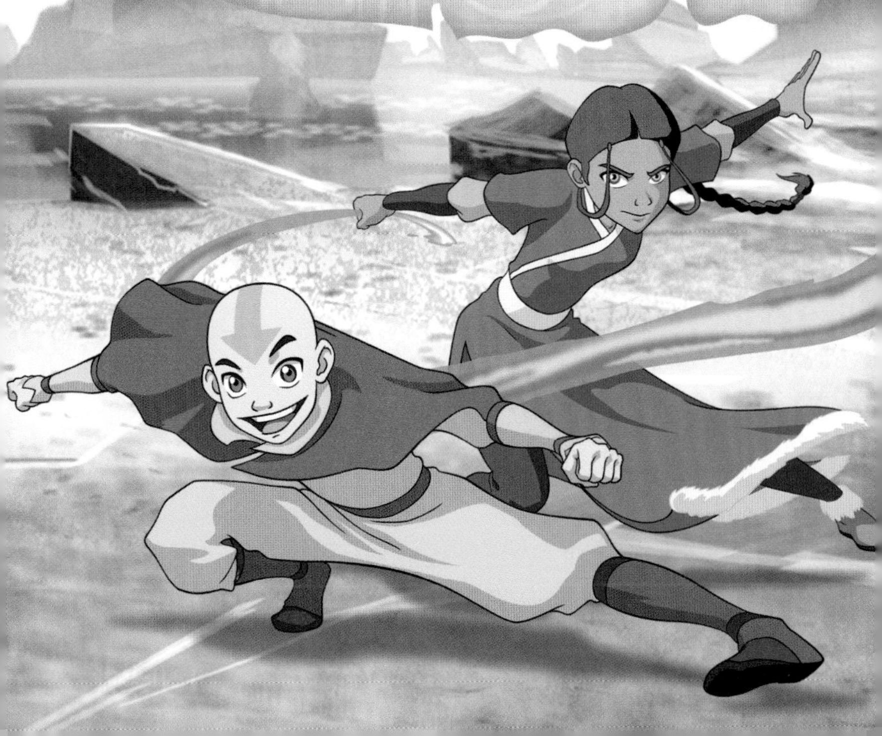

THE AVATAR RETURNS

WRITTEN BY
MICHAEL DANTE DIMARTINO
& BRYAN KONIETZKO

ADDITIONAL WRITING BY
AARON EHASZ, PETER GOLDFINGER
AND JOSH STOLBERG

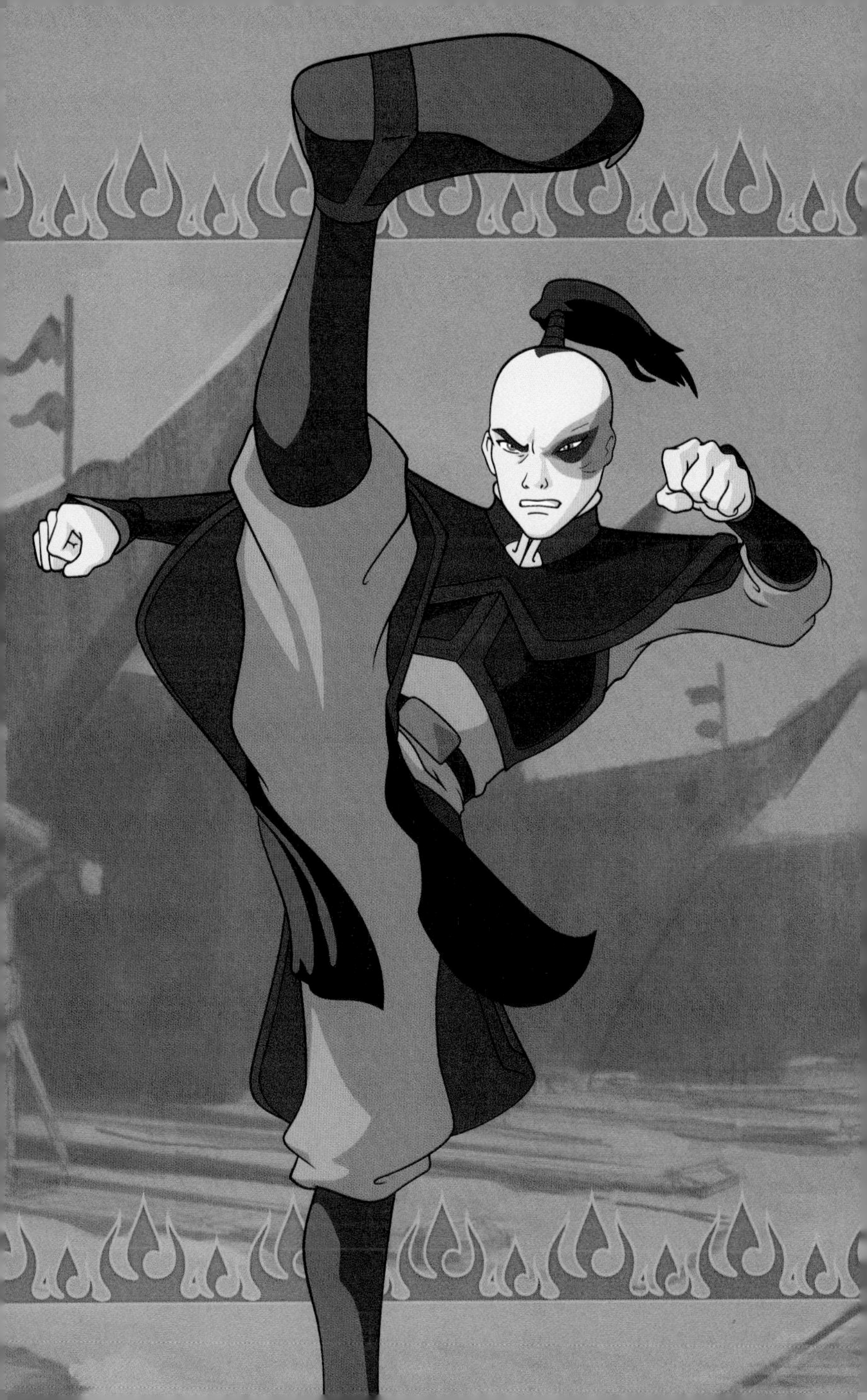

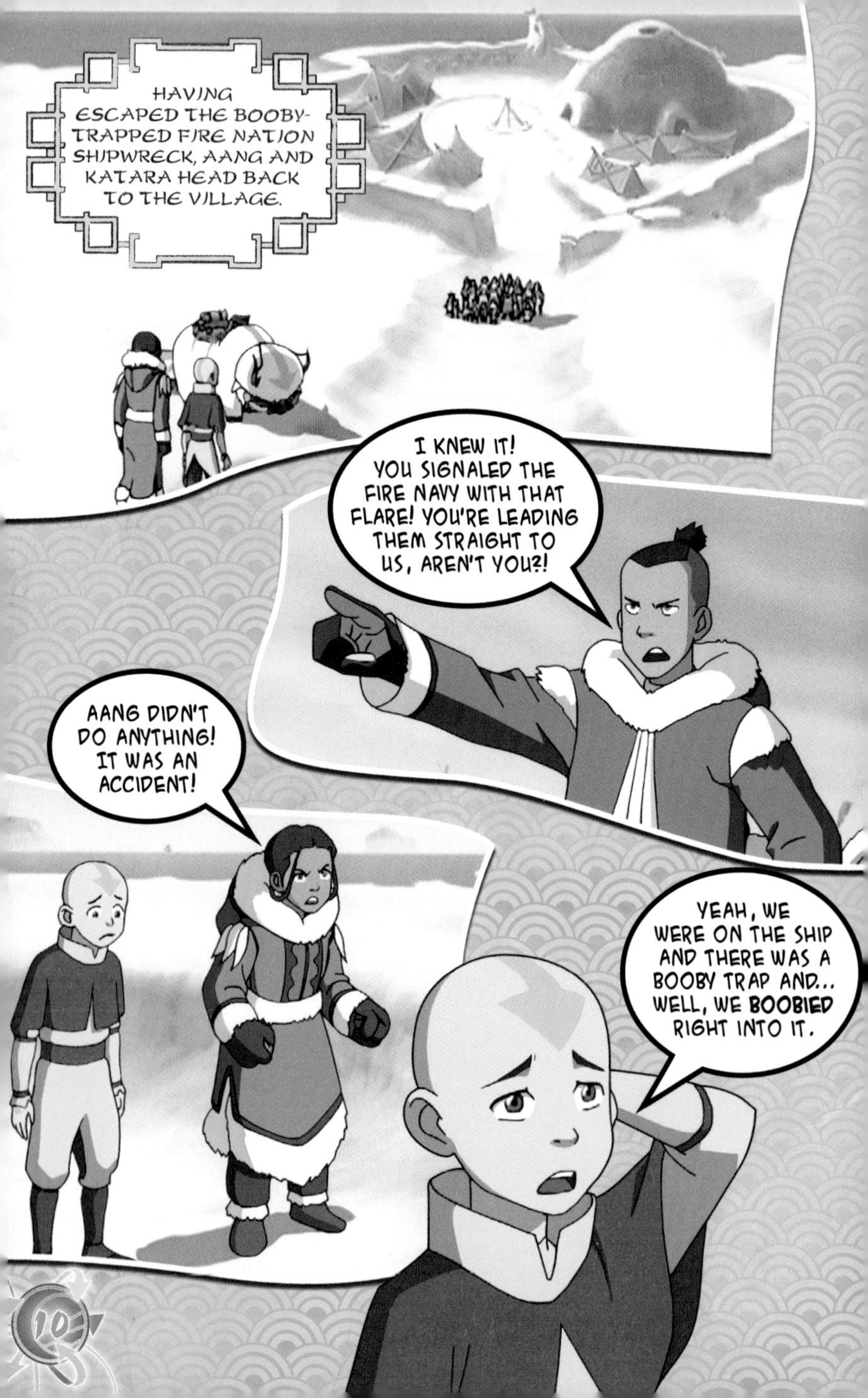
HAVING ESCAPED THE BOOBY-TRAPPED FIRE NATION SHIPWRECK, AANG AND KATARA HEAD BACK TO THE VILLAGE.
I KNEW IT! YOU SIGNALED THE FIRE NAVY WITH THAT FLARE! YOU'RE LEADING THEM STRAIGHT TO US, AREN'T YOU?!
AANG DIDN'T DO ANYTHING! IT WAS AN ACCIDENT!
YEAH, WE WERE ON THE SHIP AND THERE WAS A BOOBY TRAP AND... WELL, WE BOOBIED RIGHT INTO IT.
10

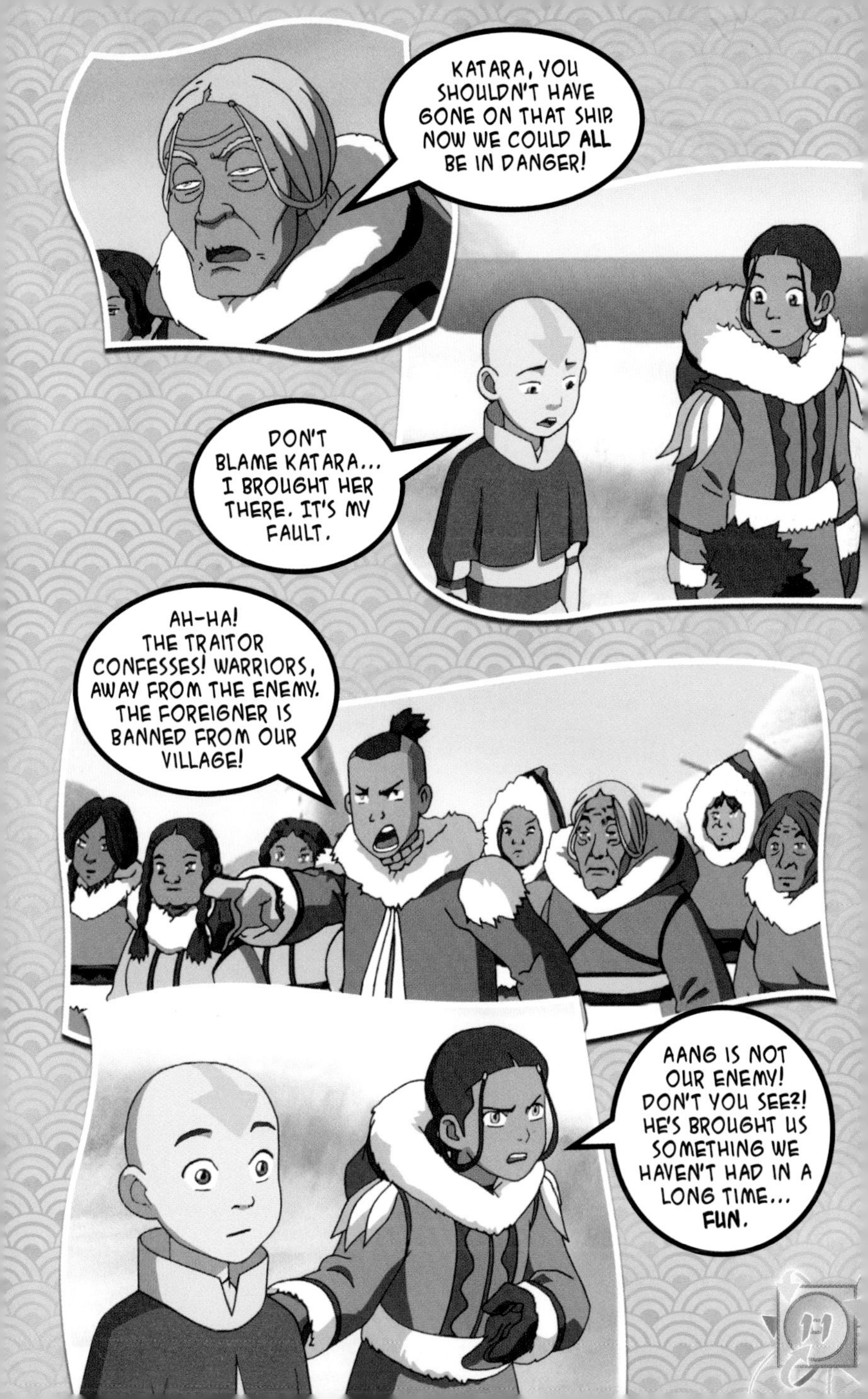
KATARA, YOU SHOULDN'T HAVE GONE ON THAT SHIP. NOW WE COULD ALL BE IN DANGER!
DON'T BLAME KATARA... I BROUGHT HER THERE. IT'S MY FAULT.
AH-HA! THE TRAITOR CONFESSES! WARRIORS, AWAY FROM THE ENEMY. THE FOREIGNER IS BANNED FROM OUR VILLAGE!
AANG IS NOT OUR ENEMY! DON'T YOU SEE?! HE'S BROUGHT US SOMETHING WE HAVEN'T HAD IN A LONG TIME... FUN.
1-1

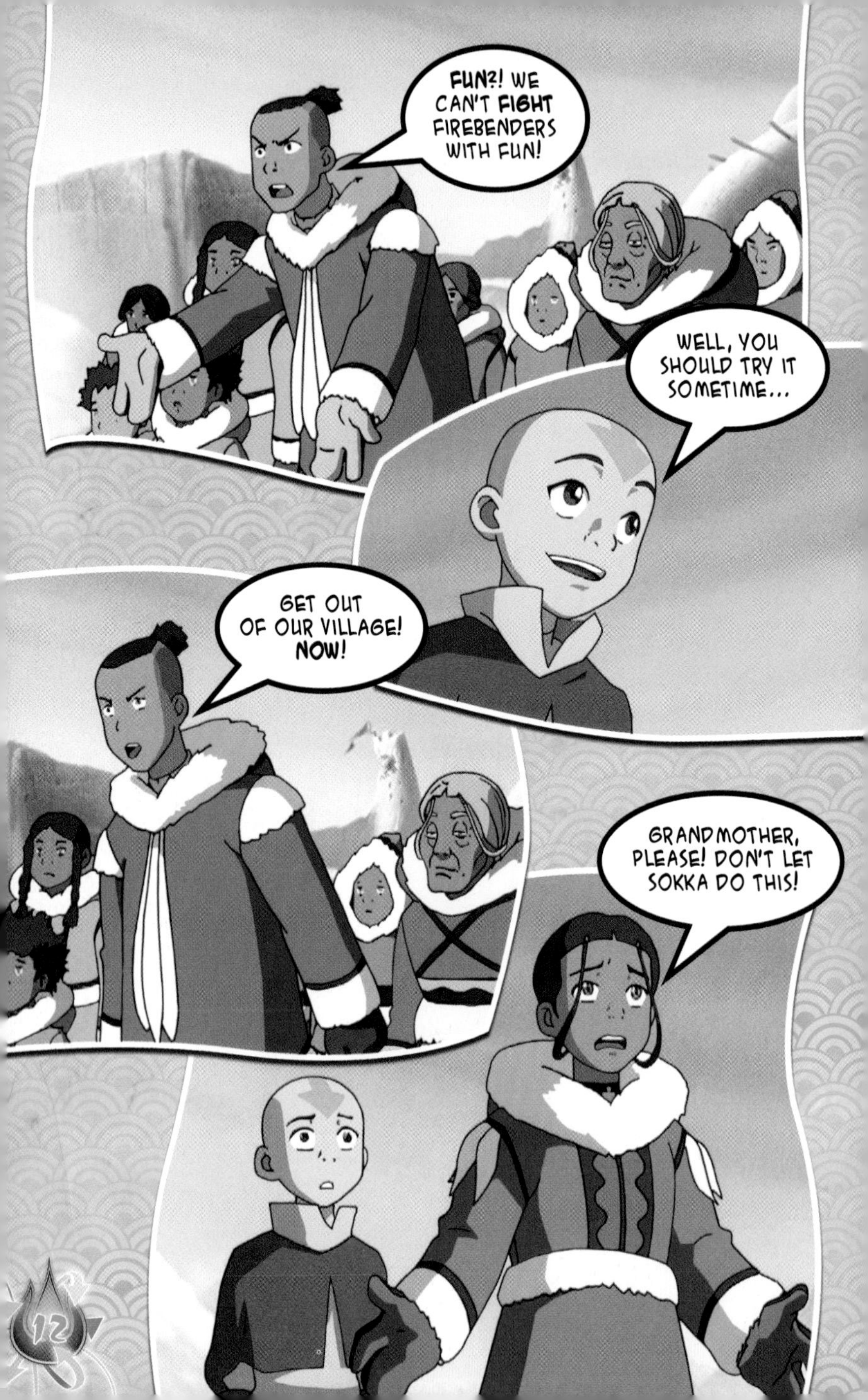
FUN?! WE CAN'T FIGHT FIREBENDERS WITH FUN!
WELL, YOU SHOULD TRY IT SOMETIME...
GET OUT OF OUR VILLAGE! NOW!
GRANDMOTHER, PLEASE! DON'T LET SOKKA DO THIS!
12

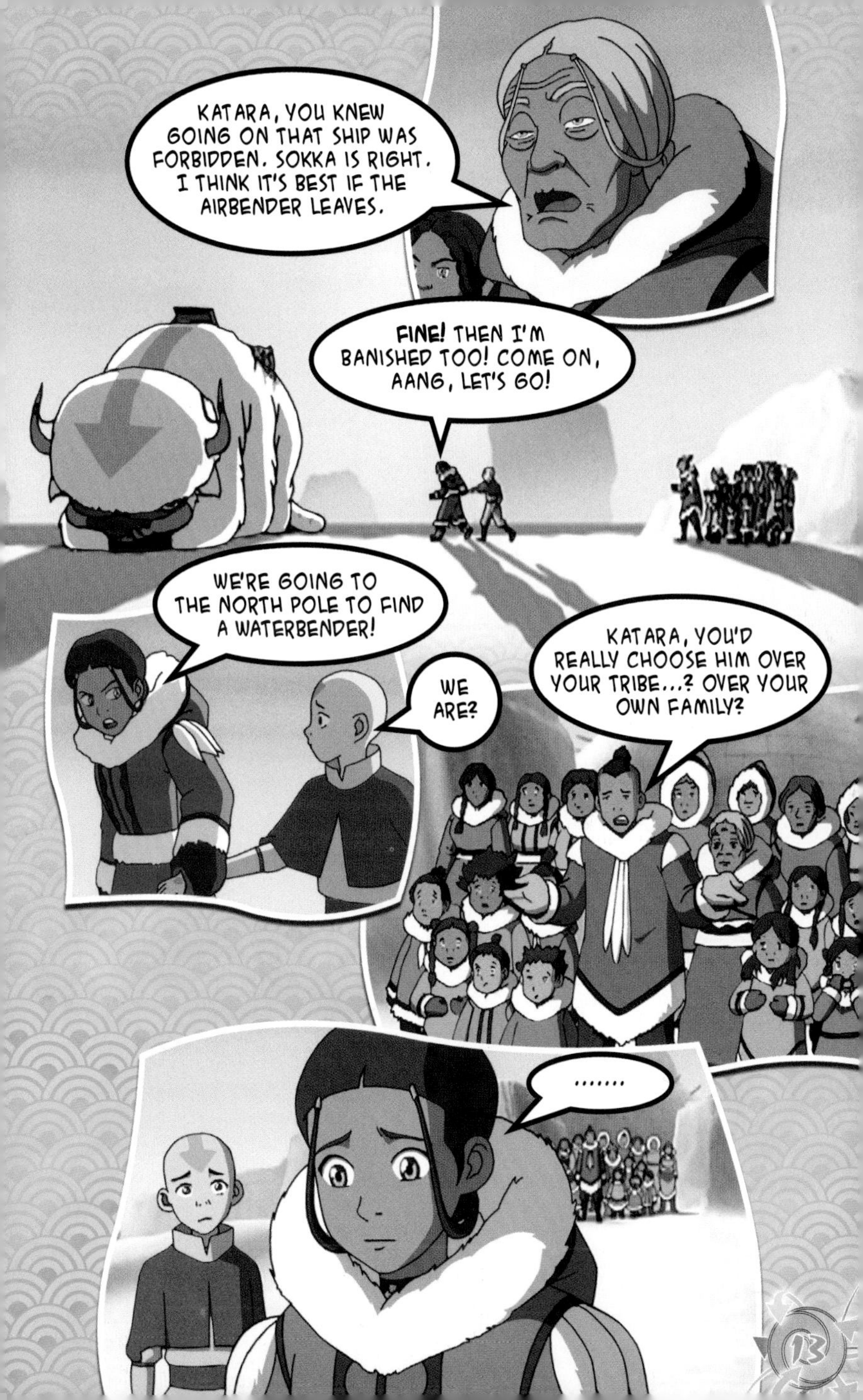
KATARA, YOU KNEW GOING ON THAT SHIP WAS FORBIDDEN. SOKKA IS RIGHT. I THINK IT'S BEST IF THE AIRBENDER LEAVES.
FINE! THEN I'M BANISHED TOO! COME ON, AANG, LET'S GO!
WE'RE GOING TO THE NORTH POLE TO FIND A WATERBENDER!
WE ARE?
KATARA, YOU'D REALLY CHOOSE HIM OVER YOUR TRIBE...? OVER YOUR OWN FAMILY?
....

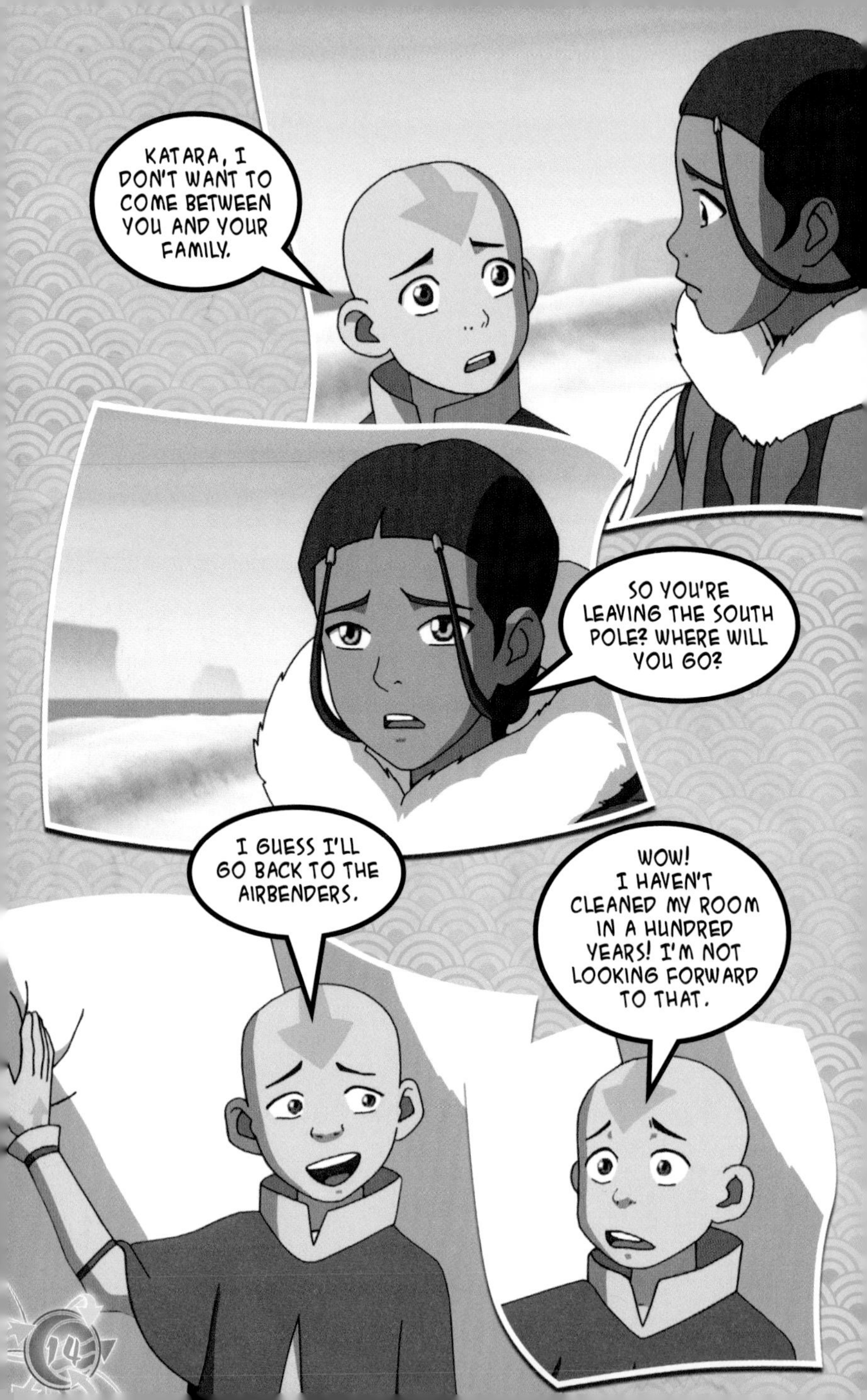
KATARA, I DON'T WANT TO COME BETWEEN YOU AND YOUR FAMILY.
SO YOU'RE LEAVING THE SOUTH POLE? WHERE WILL YOU GO?
I GUESS I'LL GO BACK TO THE AIRBENDERS.
WOW! I HAVEN'T CLEANED MY ROOM IN A HUNDRED YEARS! I'M NOT LOOKING FORWARD TO THAT.

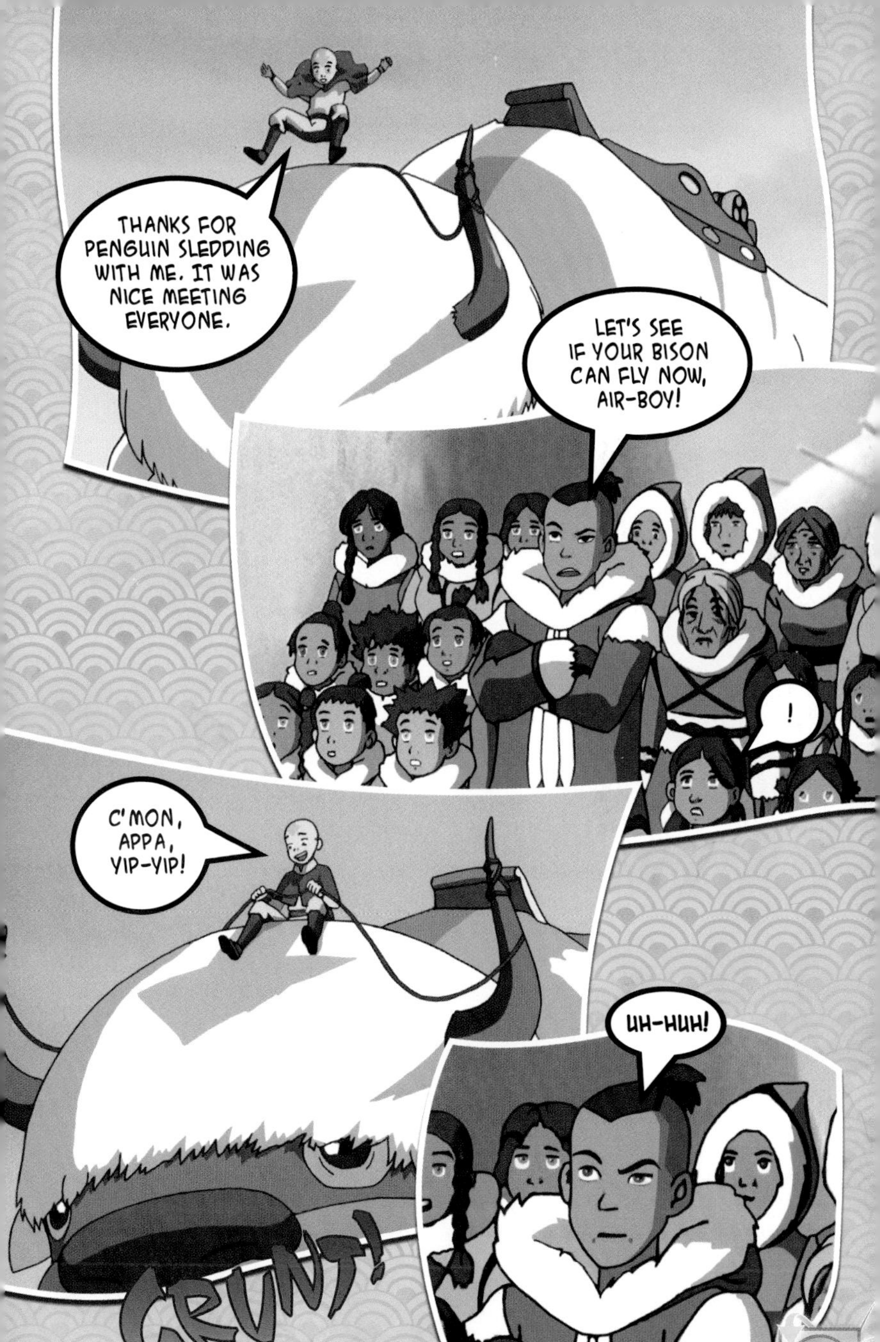
THANKS FOR PENGUIN SLEDDING WITH ME. IT WAS NICE MEETING EVERYONE.
LET'S SEE IF YOUR BISON CAN FLY NOW, AIR-BOY!
!
C'MON, APPA, YIP-YIP!
GRUNT!
UH-HUH!

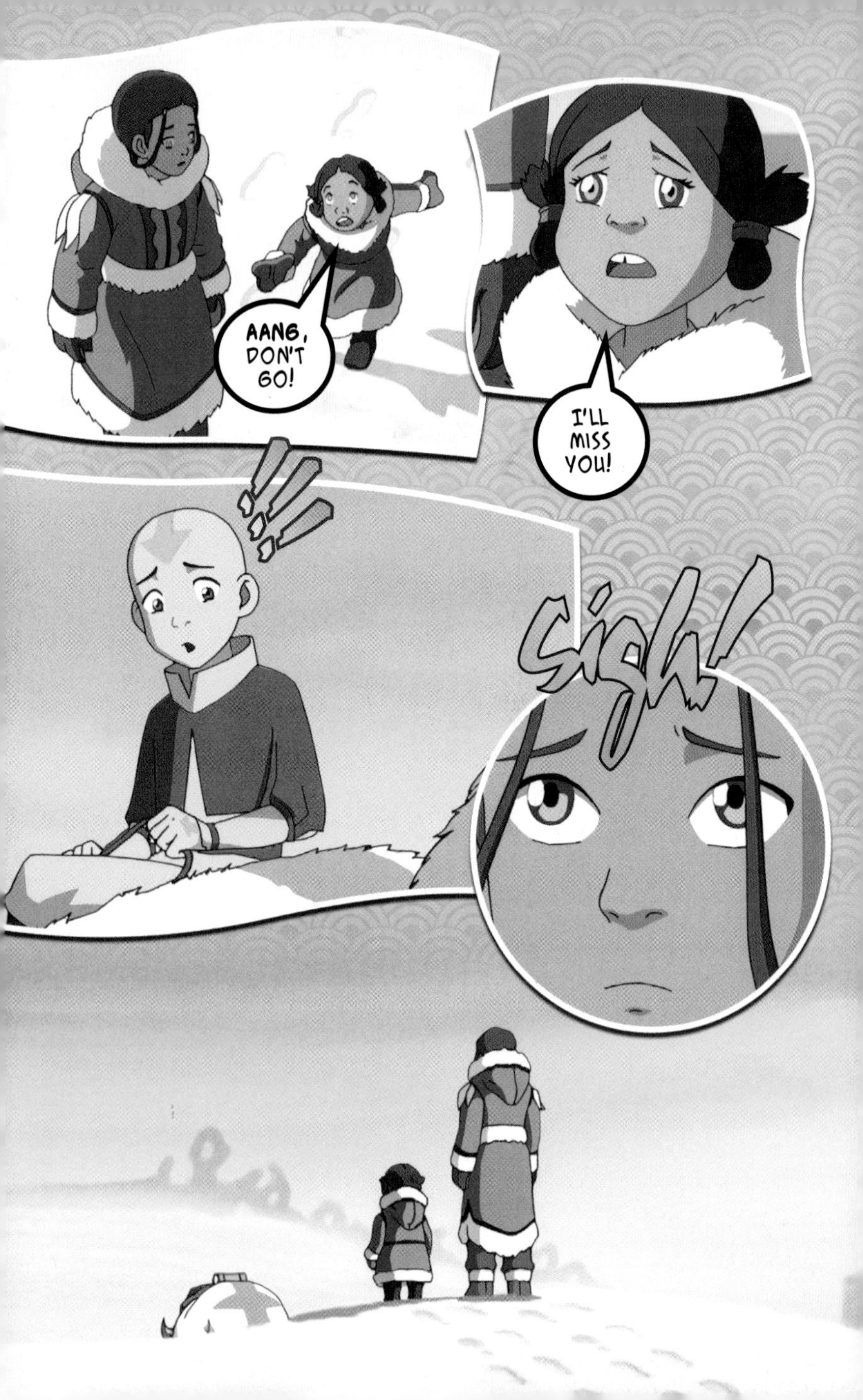
AANG, DON'T GO!
I'LL MISS YOU!
Sigh!

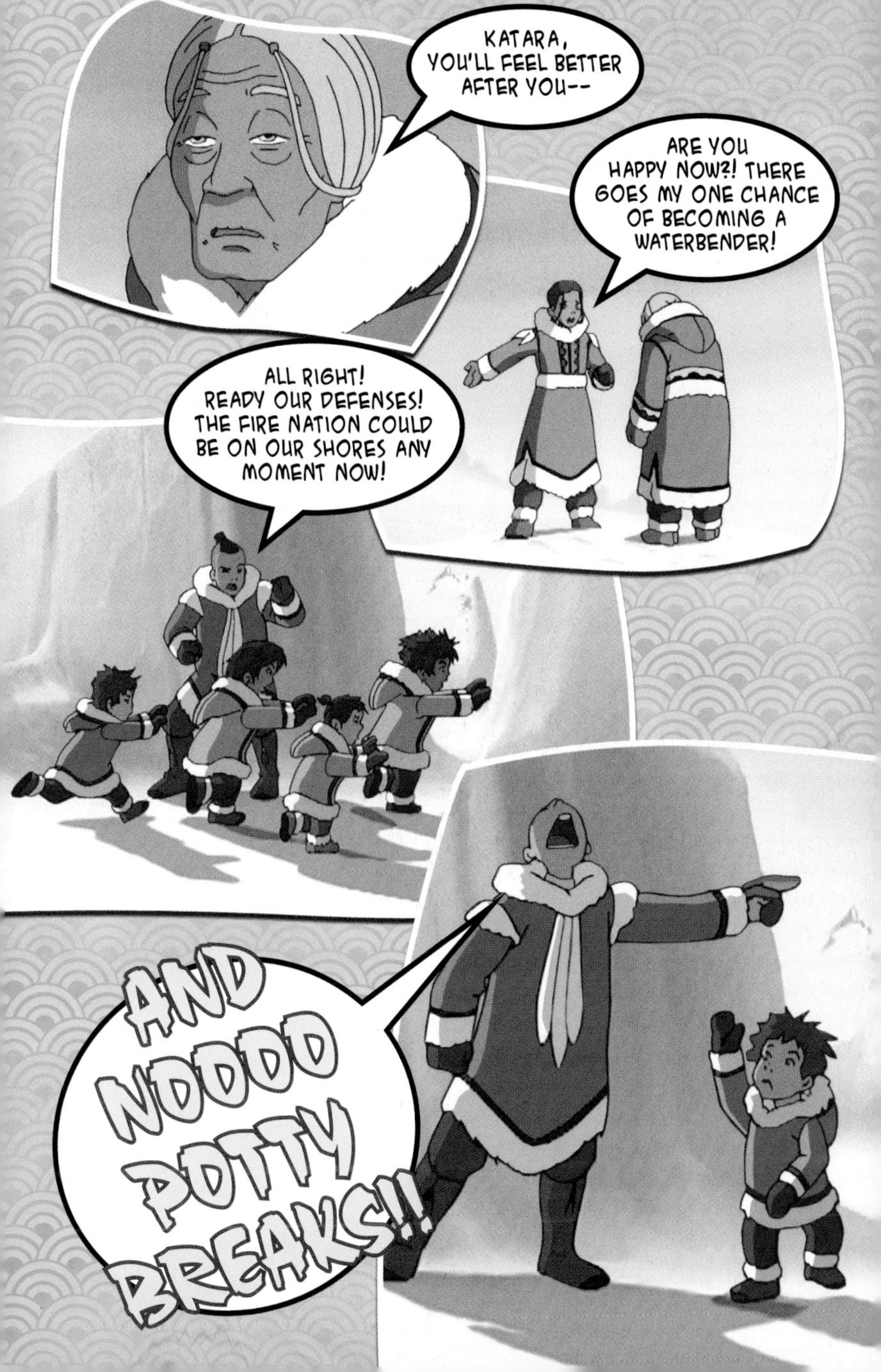
KATARA, YOU'LL FEEL BETTER AFTER YOU--
ARE YOU HAPPY NOW?! THERE GOES MY ONE CHANCE OF BECOMING A WATERBENDER!
ALL RIGHT! READY OUR DEFENSES! THE FIRE NATION COULD BE ON OUR SHORES ANY MOMENT NOW!
AND NOOOO POTTY BREAKS!!

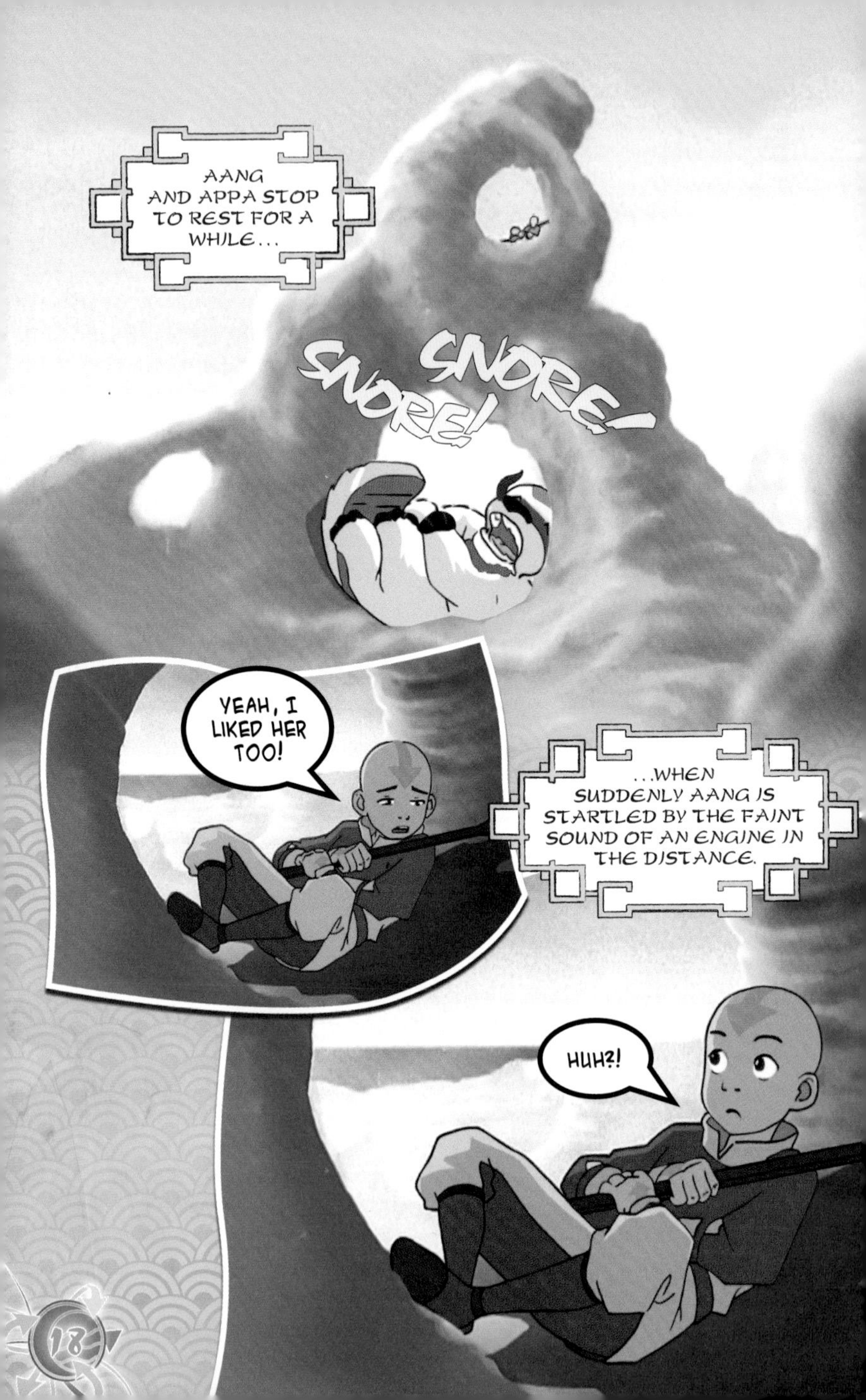
AANG AND APPA STOP TO REST FOR A WHILE...
SNORE! SNORE!
YEAH, I LIKED HER TOO!
...WHEN SUDDENLY AANG IS STARTLED BY THE FAINT SOUND OF AN ENGINE IN THE DISTANCE.
HUH?!

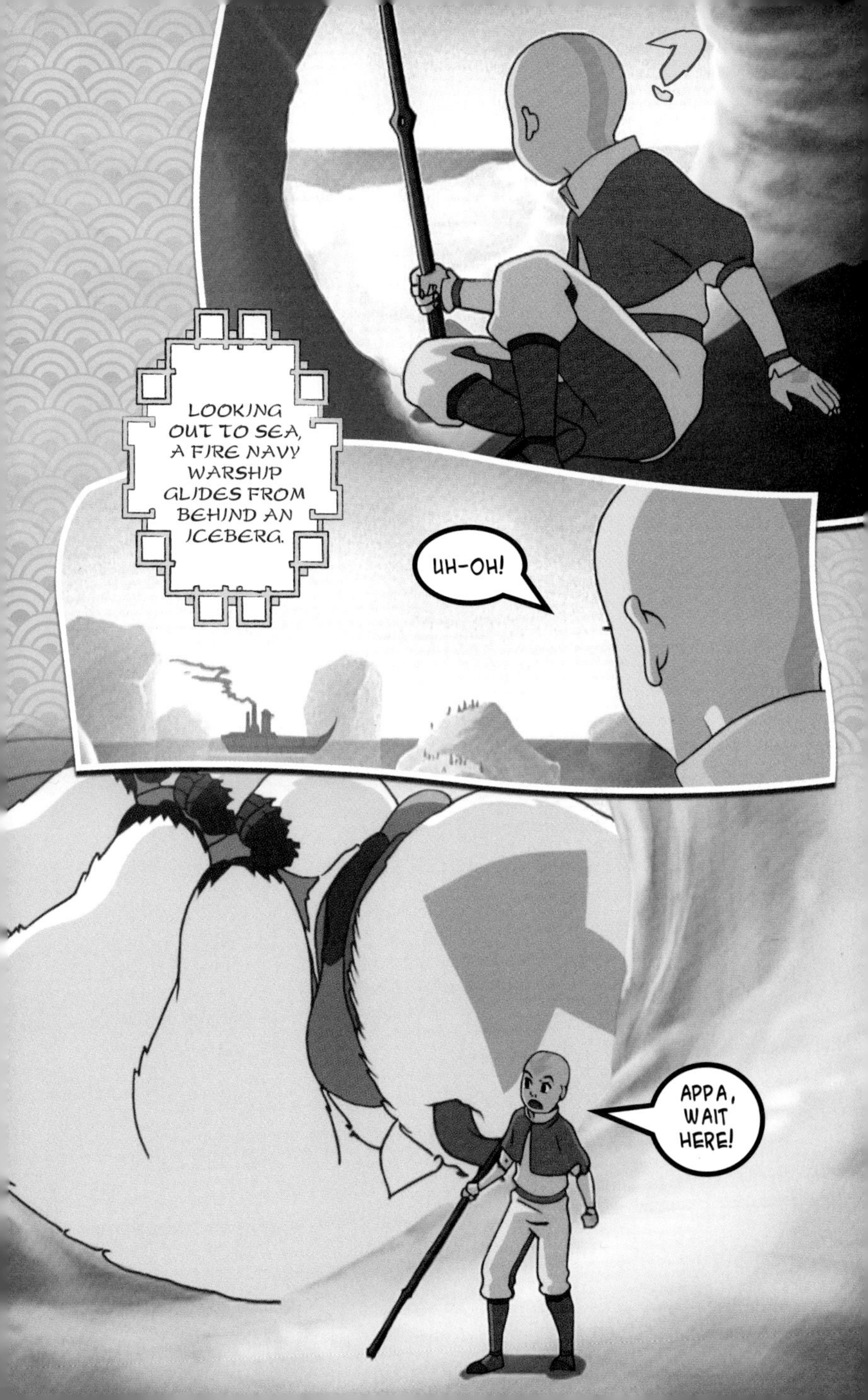
LOOKING OUT TO SEA, A FIRE NAVY WARSHIP GLIDES FROM BEHIND AN ICEBERG.
UH-OH!
APPA, WAIT HERE!

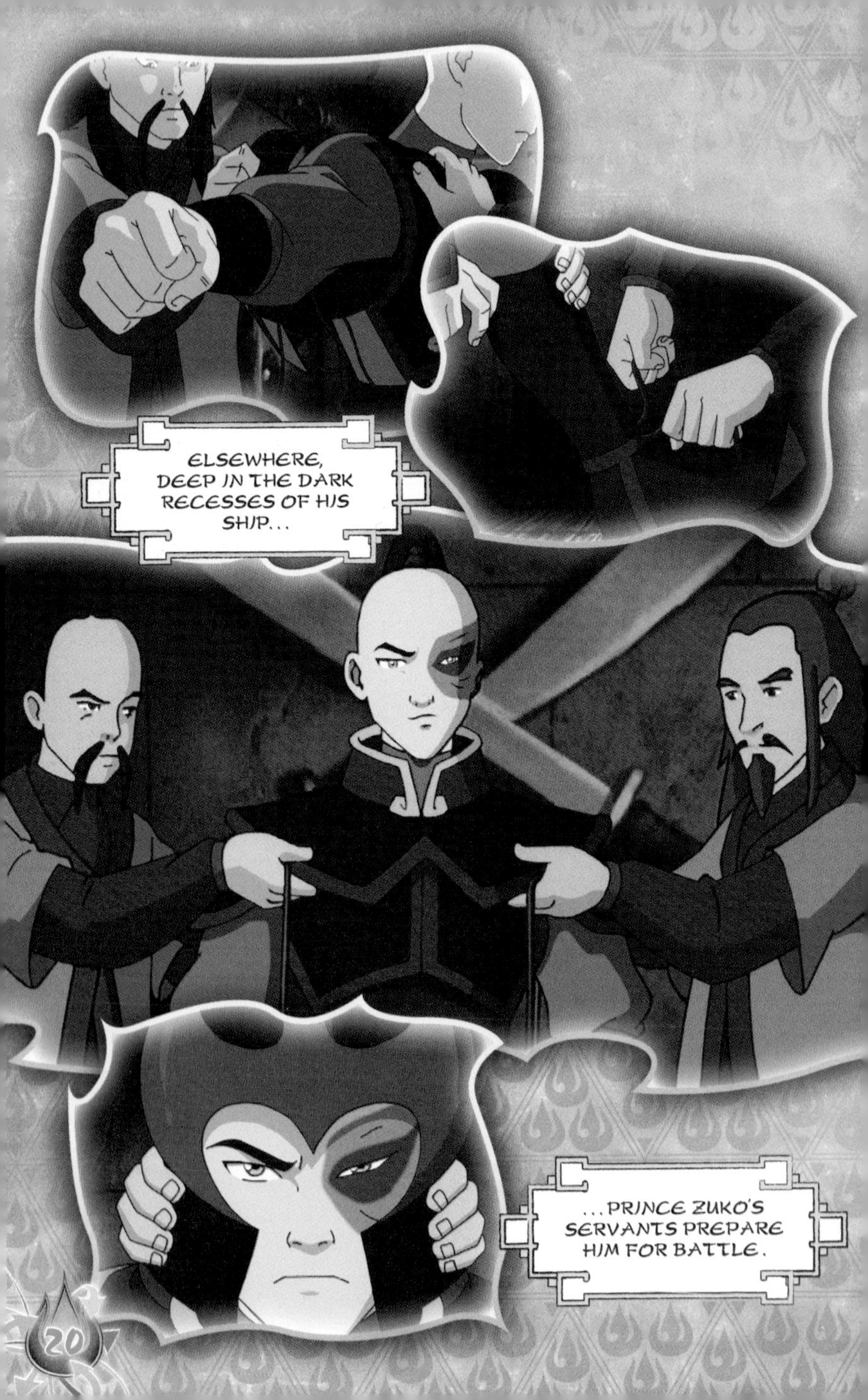
ELSEWHERE, DEEP IN THE DARK RECESSES OF HIS SHIP...
...PRINCE ZUKO'S SERVANTS PREPARE HIM FOR BATTLE.

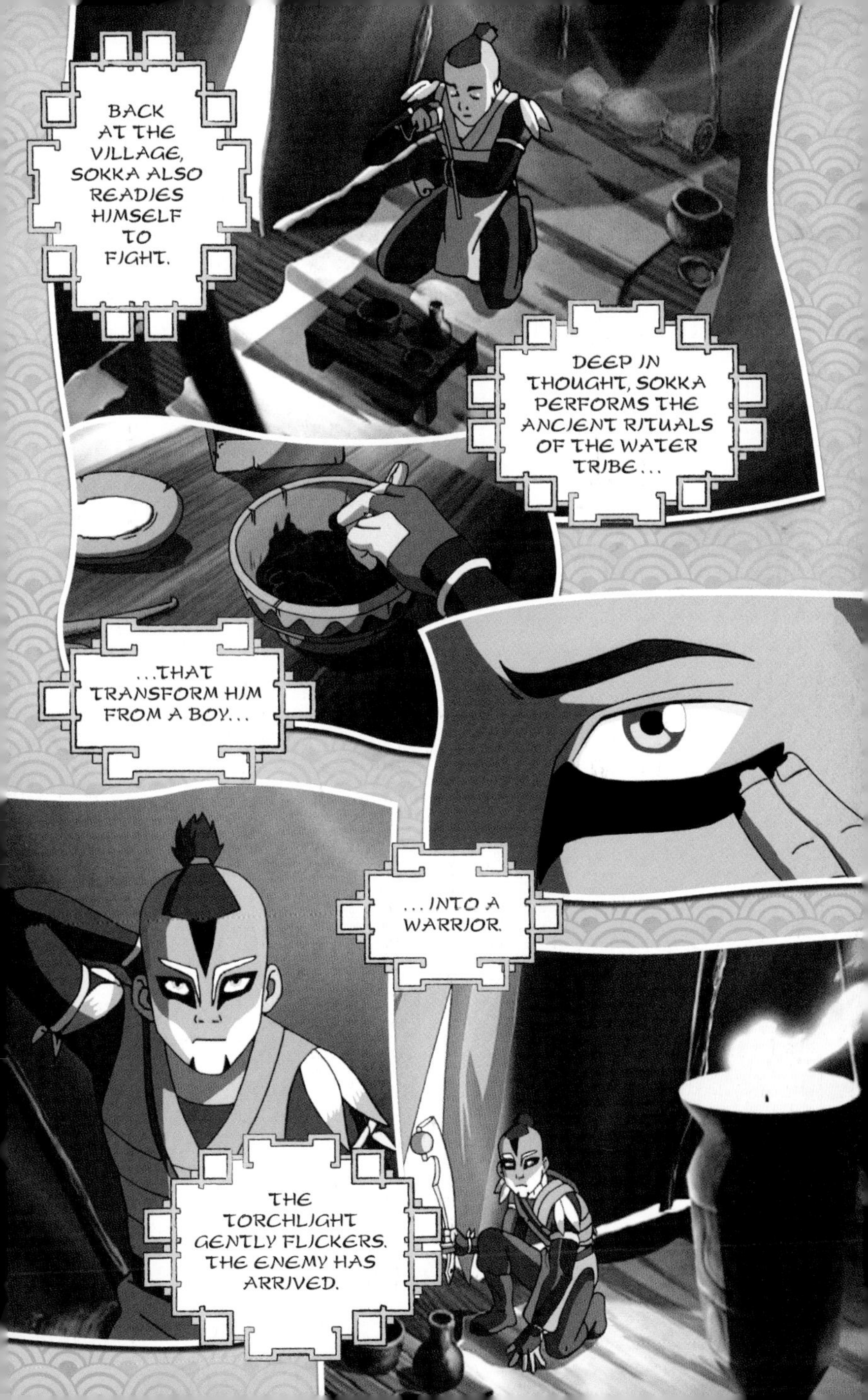
BACK AT THE VILLAGE, SOKKA ALSO READIES HIMSELF TO FIGHT.
DEEP IN THOUGHT, SOKKA PERFORMS THE ANCIENT RITUALS OF THE WATER TRIBE...
...THAT TRANSFORM HIM FROM A BOY...
...INTO A WARRIOR.
THE TORCHLIGHT GENTLY FLICKERS. THE ENEMY HAS ARRIVED.

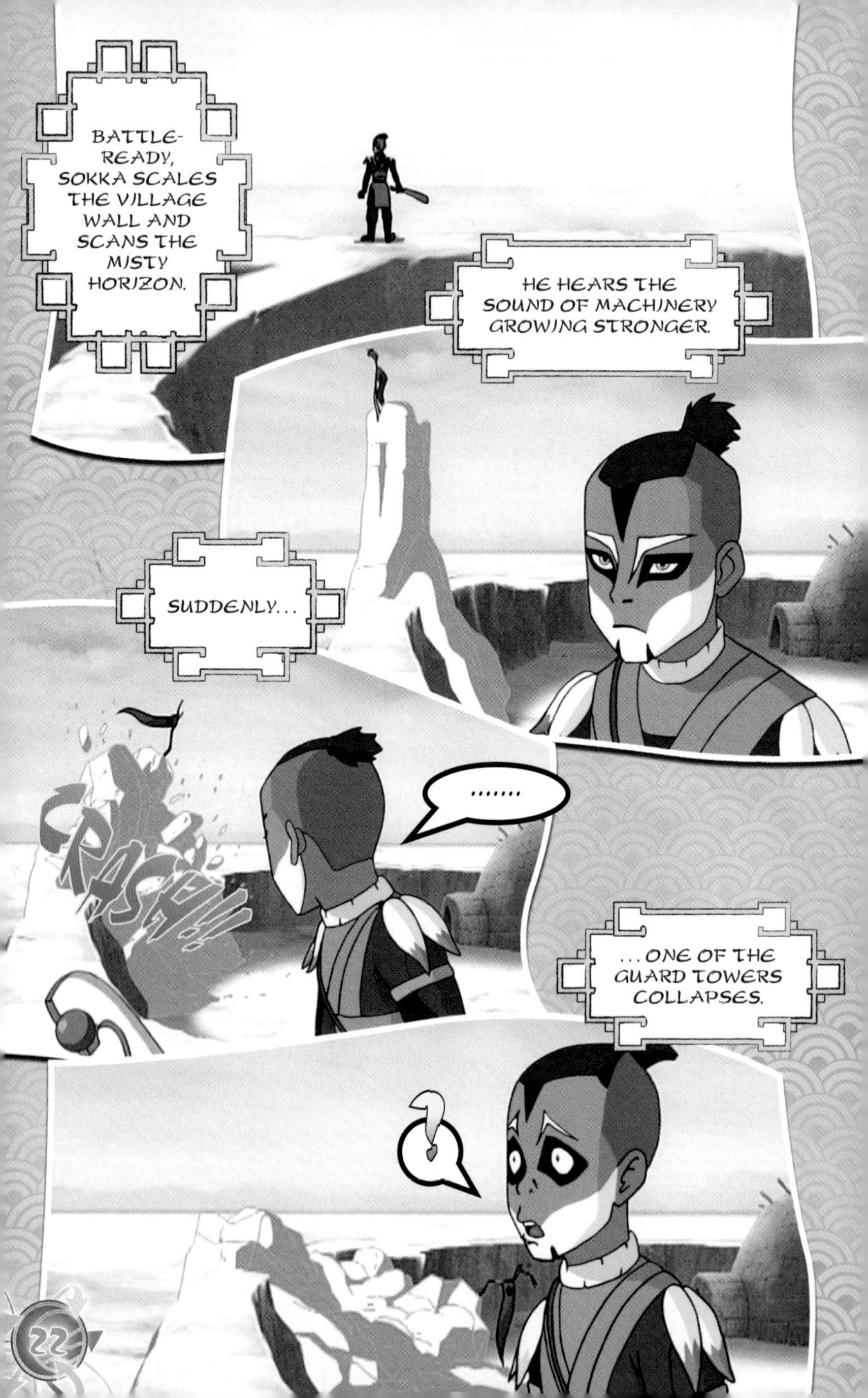
BATTLE-READY, SOKKA SCALES THE VILLAGE WALL AND SCANS THE MISTY HORIZON.
HE HEARS THE SOUND OF MACHINERY GROWING STRONGER.
SUDDENLY...
CRASH!!
....
...ONE OF THE GUARD TOWERS COLLAPSES.
?

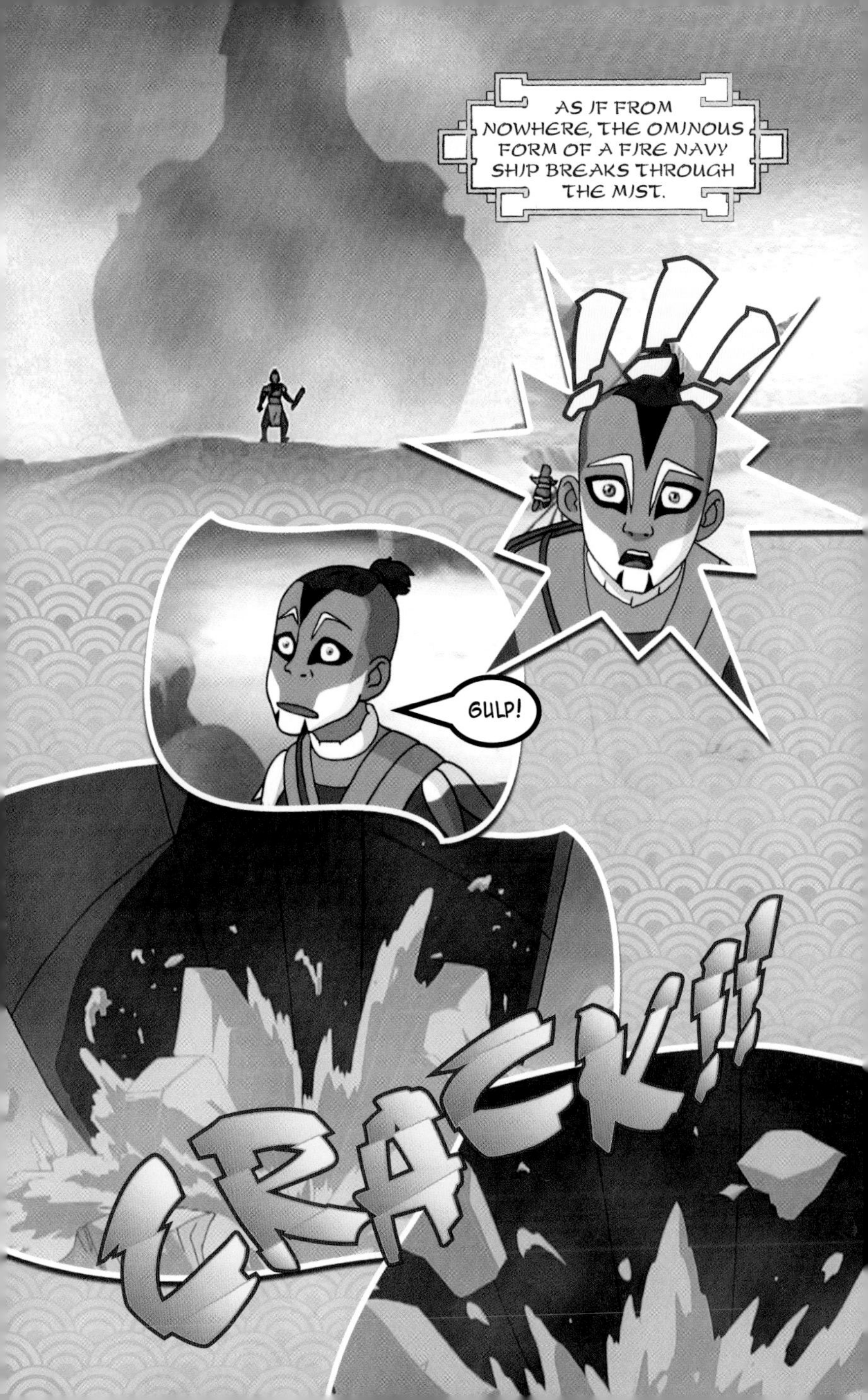
AS IF FROM NOWHERE, THE OMINOUS FORM OF A FIRE NAVY SHIP BREAKS THROUGH THE MIST.
GULP!
CRACK!!

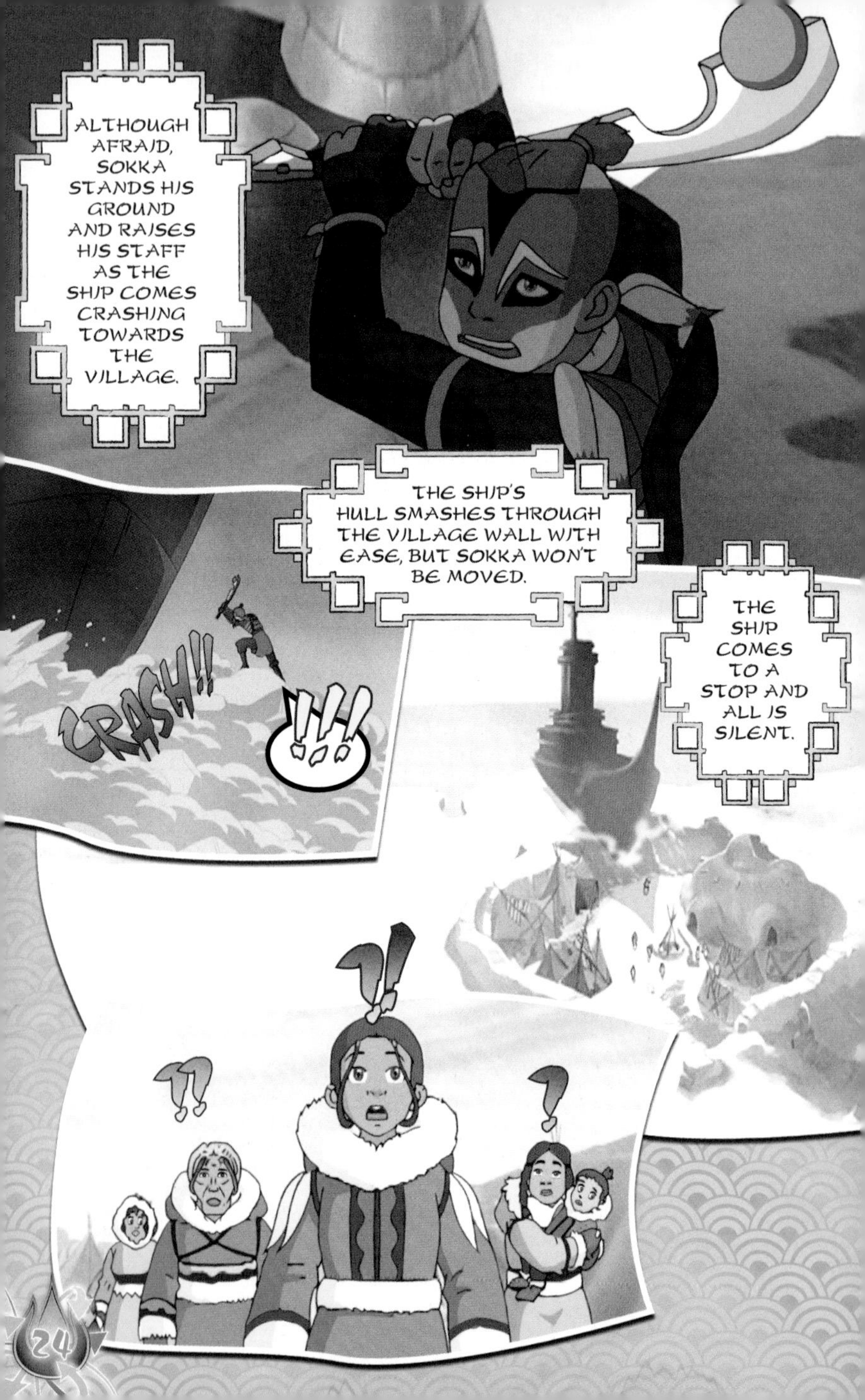
ALTHOUGH AFRAID, SOKKA STANDS HIS GROUND AND RAISES HIS STAFF AS THE SHIP COMES CRASHING TOWARDS THE VILLAGE.
THE SHIP'S HULL SMASHES THROUGH THE VILLAGE WALL WITH EASE, BUT SOKKA WON'T BE MOVED.
CRASH!!
!!!
THE SHIP COMES TO A STOP AND ALL IS SILENT.

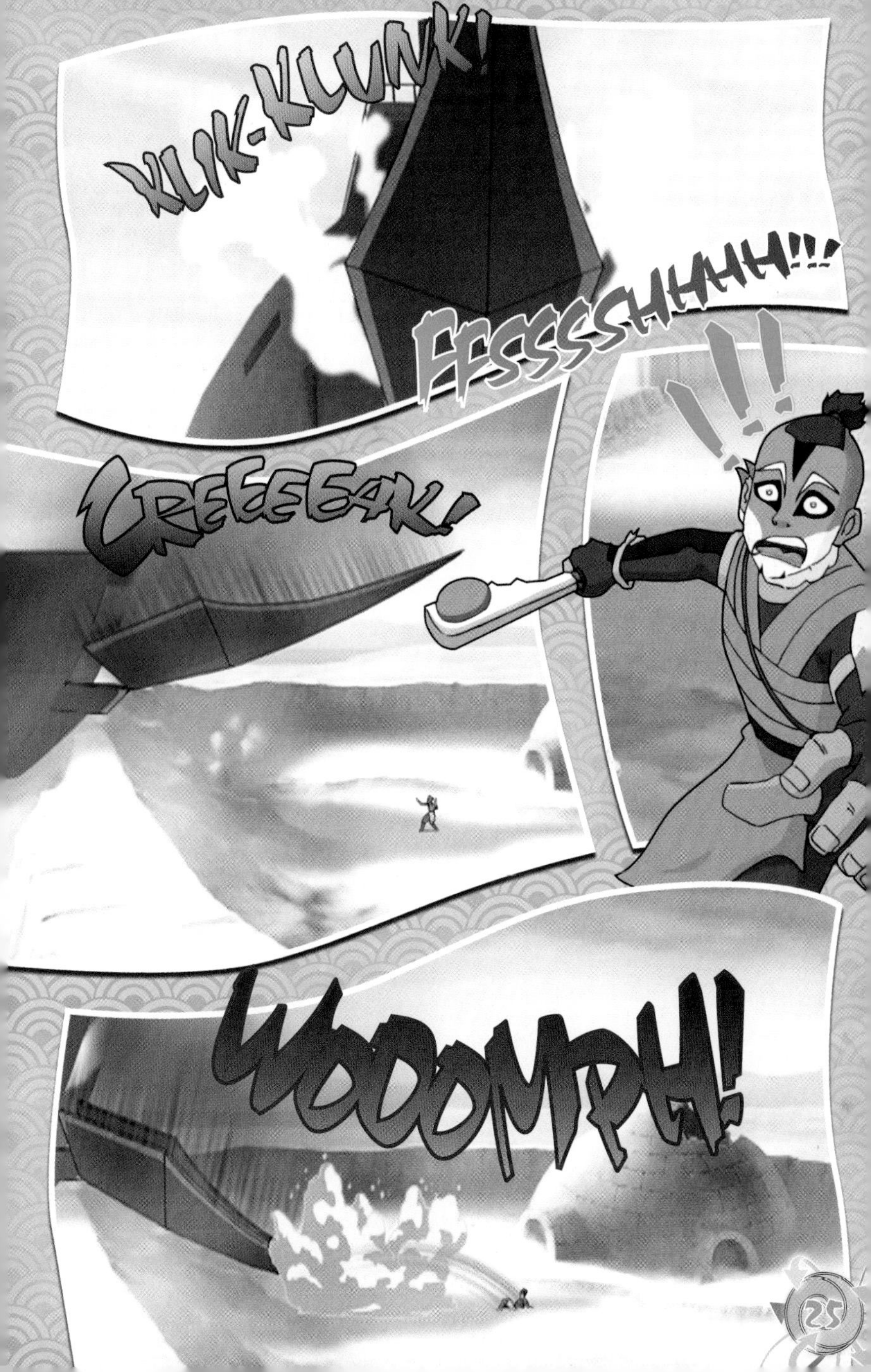
KLIK-KLUNK!
FFSSSSHHHHH!!!
!!!
CREEEEAK!
WOOOMPH!

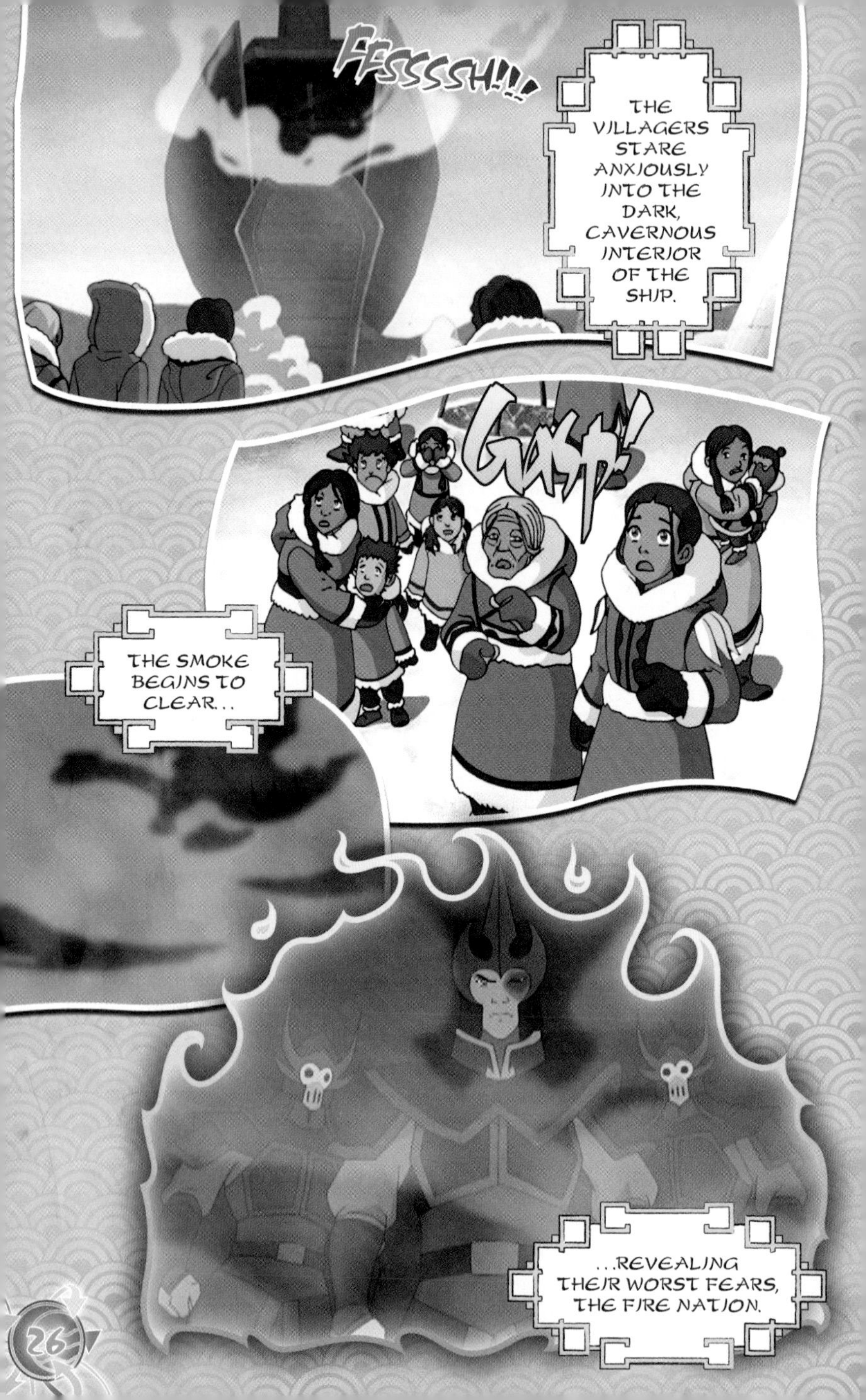
FSSSSH!!!
THE VILLAGERS STARE ANXIOUSLY INTO THE DARK, CAVERNOUS INTERIOR OF THE SHIP.
GASP!
THE SMOKE BEGINS TO CLEAR...
...REVEALING THEIR WORST FEARS, THE FIRE NATION.

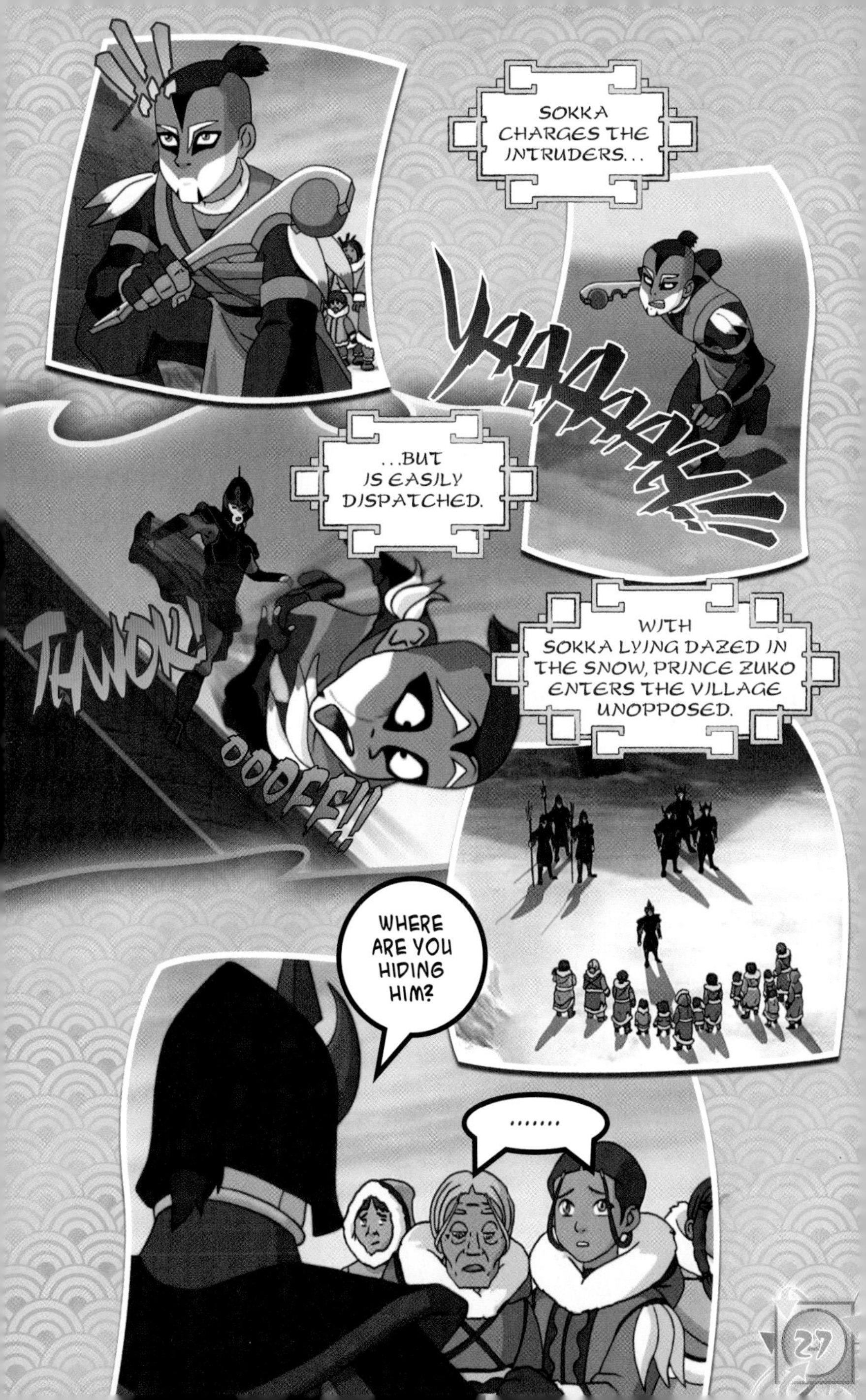
SOKKA CHARGES THE INTRUDERS...
YAAAAAAK!!!
...BUT IS EASILY DISPATCHED.
THWOK!
OOOFF!!
WITH SOKKA LYING DAZED IN THE SNOW, PRINCE ZUKO ENTERS THE VILLAGE UNOPPOSED.
WHERE ARE YOU HIDING HIM?
....

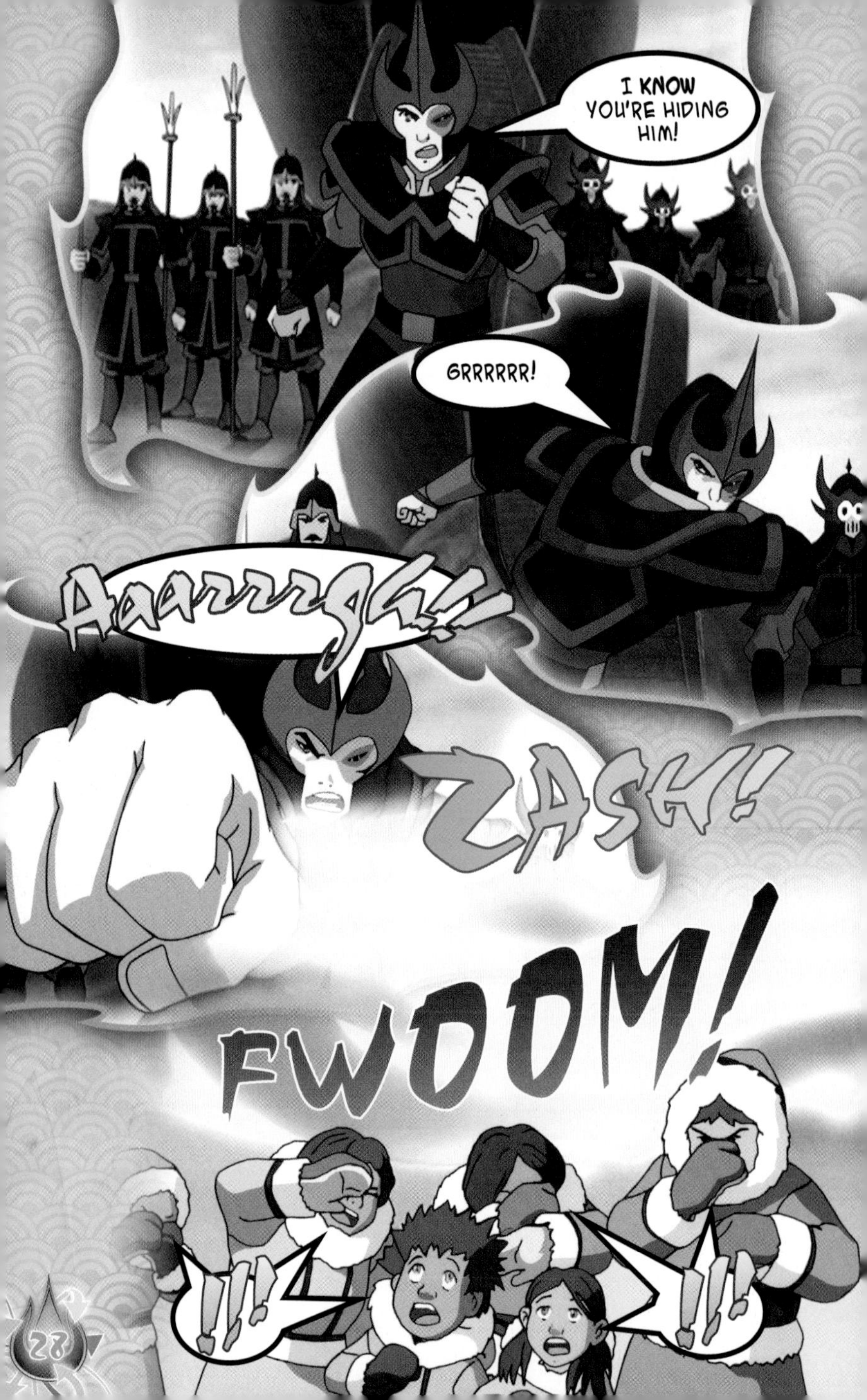
I KNOW YOU'RE HIDING HIM!
GRRRRRR!
Aaarrrgh!!
ZASH!
FWOOM!
!!
!!

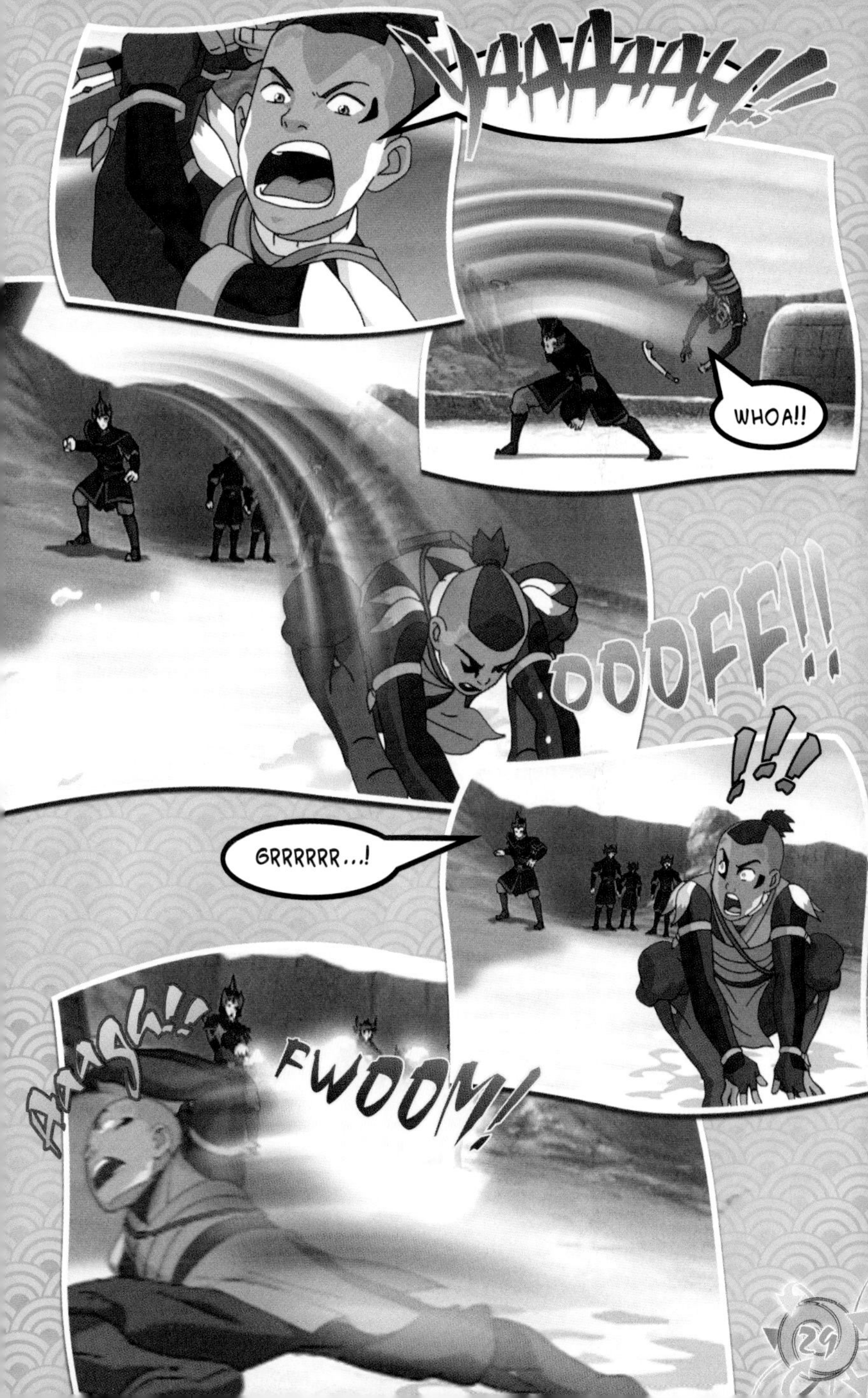

YAAAAAH!!
WHOA!!
OOOFF!!
!!!
GRRRRRR...!
AAAGH!!
FWOOM!

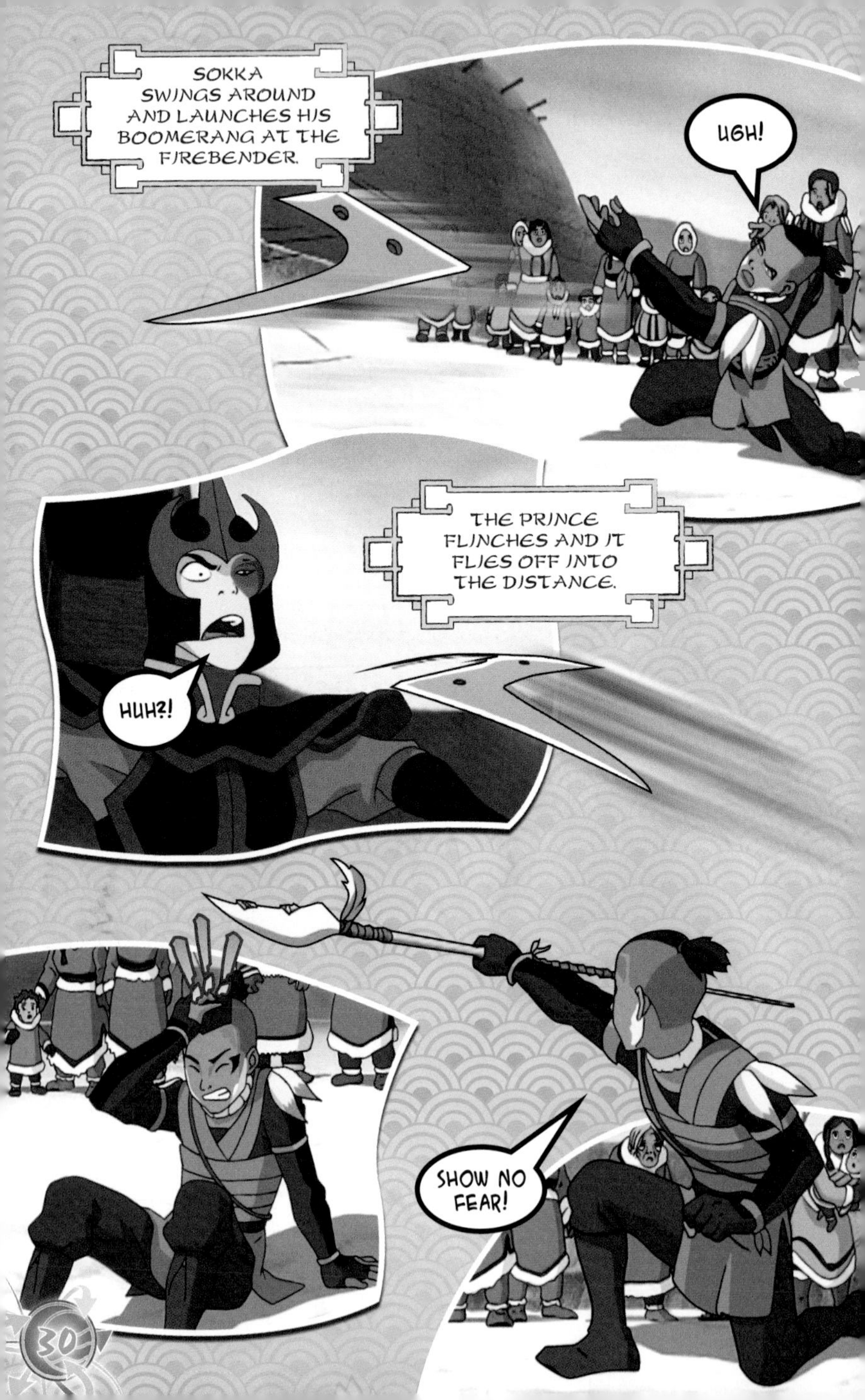
SOKKA SWINGS AROUND AND LAUNCHES HIS BOOMERANG AT THE FIREBENDER.
UGH!
THE PRINCE FLINCHES AND IT FLIES OFF INTO THE DISTANCE.
HUH?!
SHOW NO FEAR!

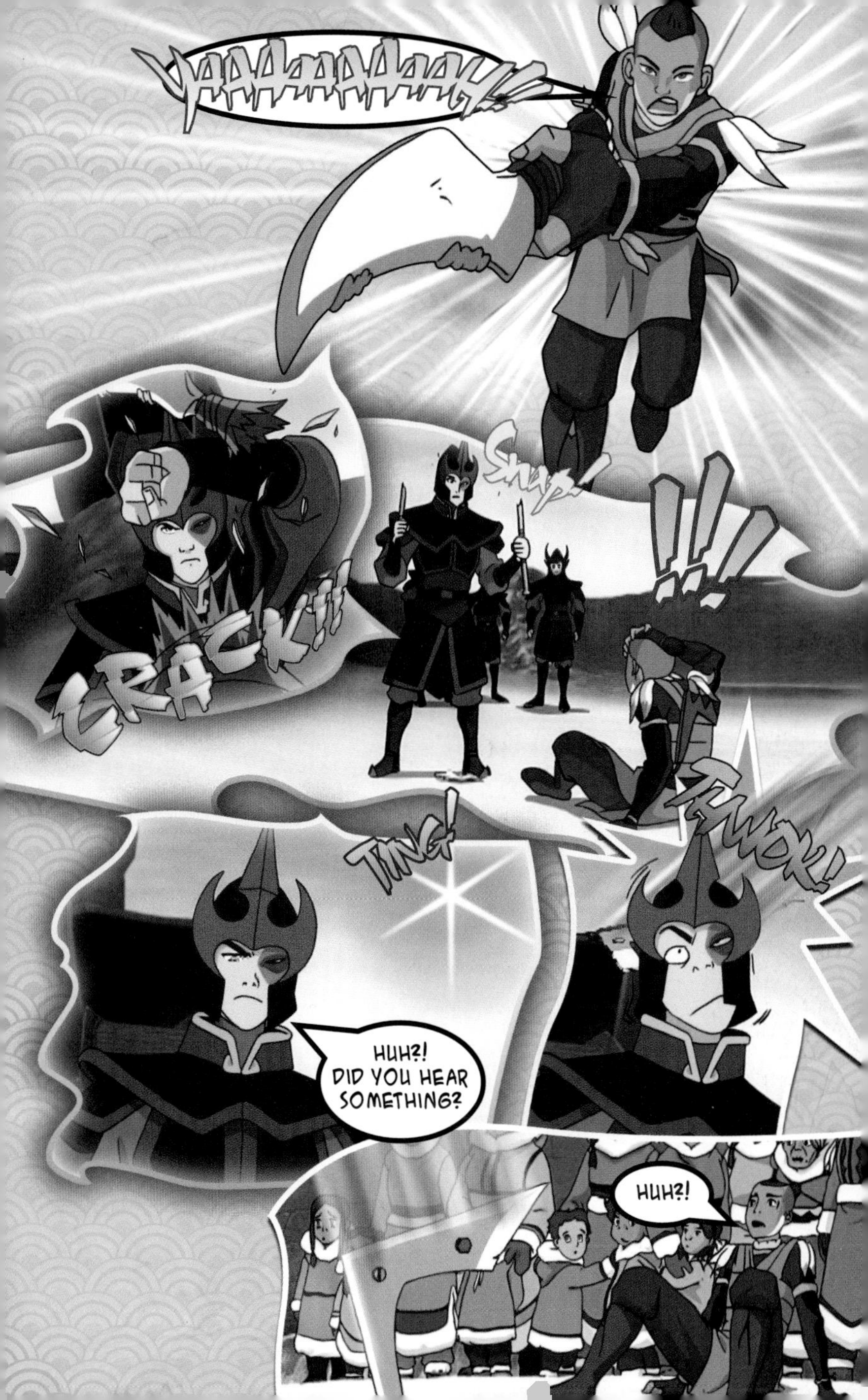
YAAAAAAAAAAH!!!
SNAP!
CRACK!!!
!!!!
TING!
THWOCK!
HUH?!
DID YOU HEAR
SOMETHING?
HUH?!

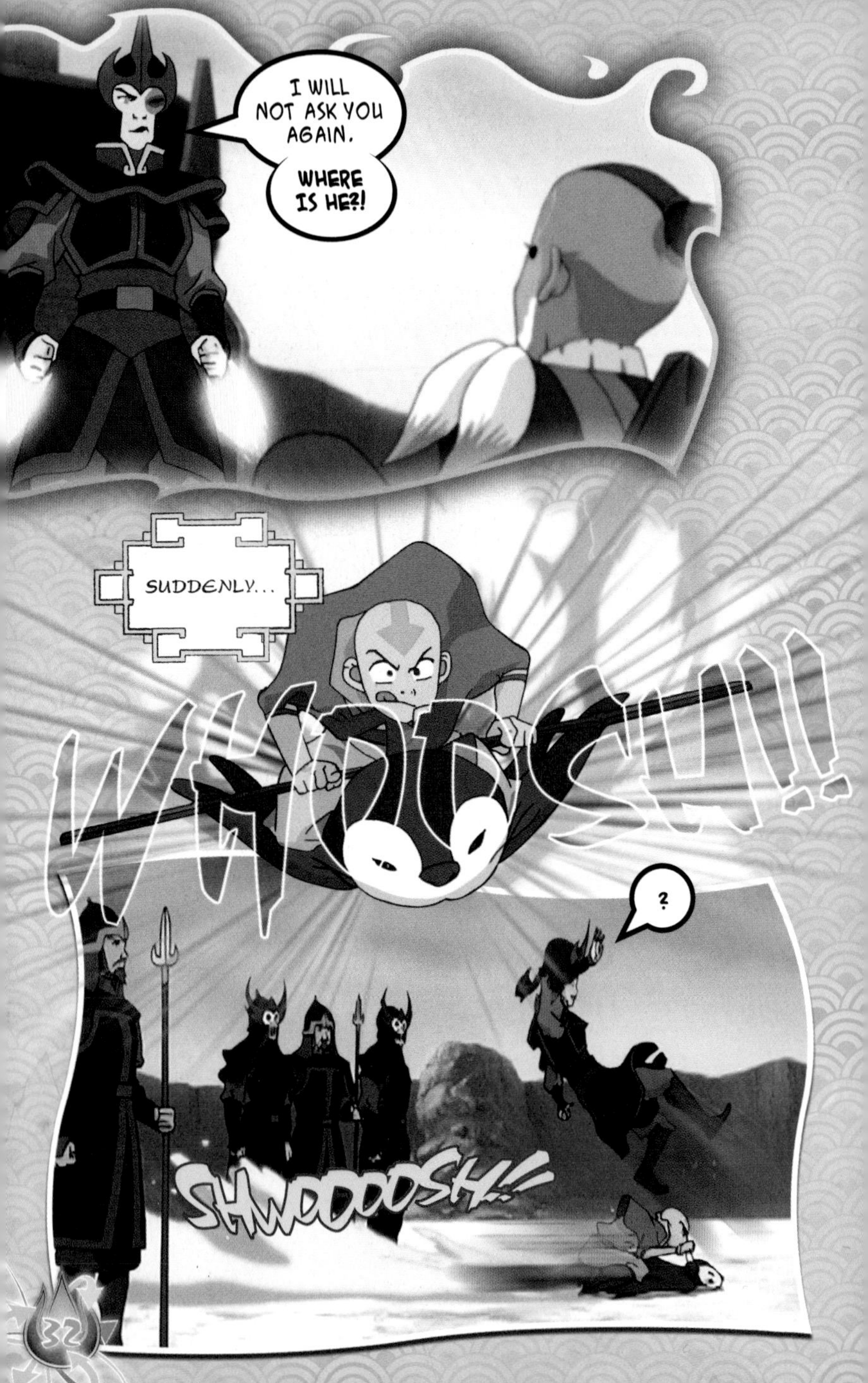
I WILL NOT ASK YOU AGAIN.
WHERE IS HE?!
SUDDENLY...
WHOOSH!!
?
SHWOOOOSH!!

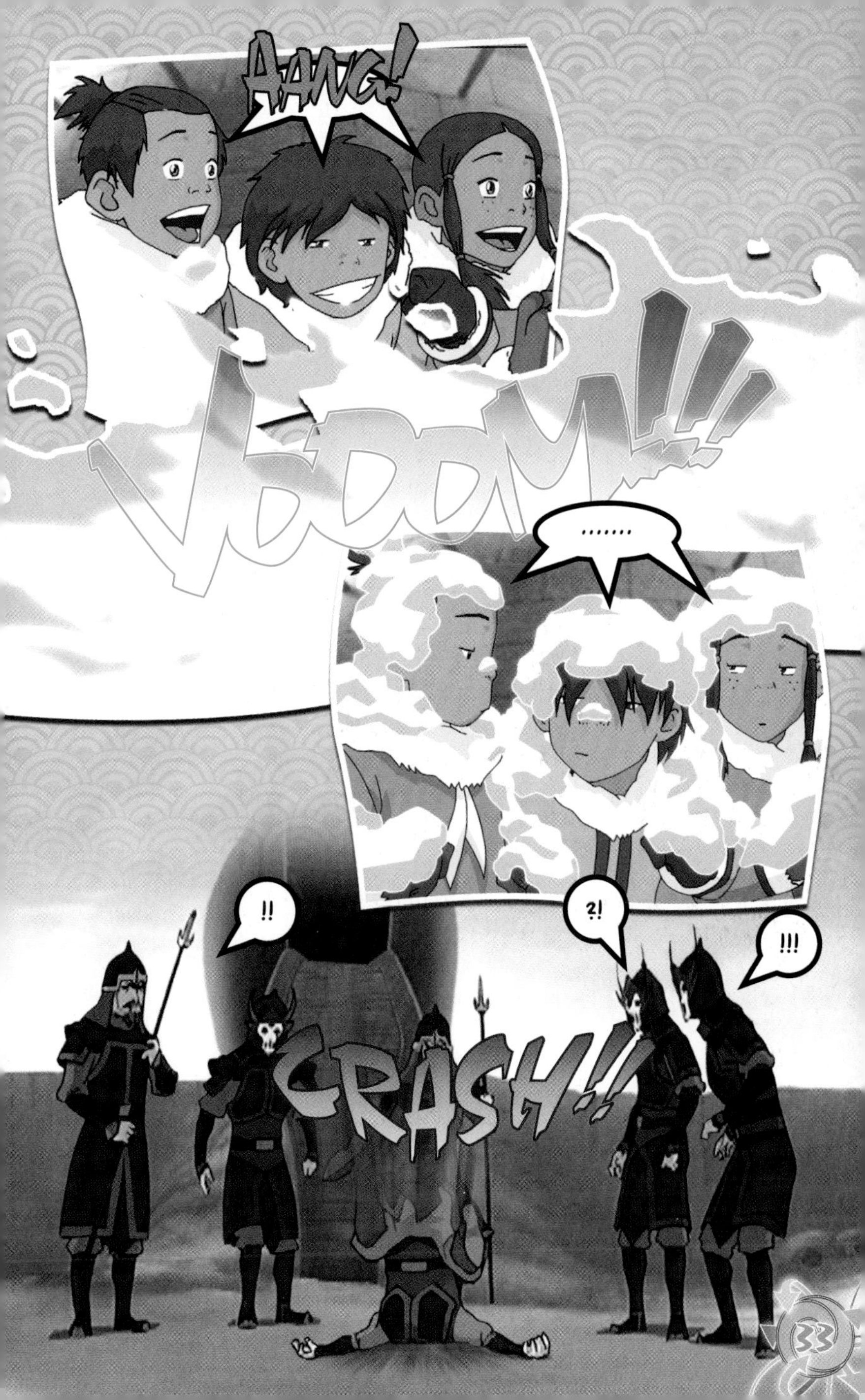
AANG!
VOOOM!!!
....
!!
?!
!!!
CRASH!!
33

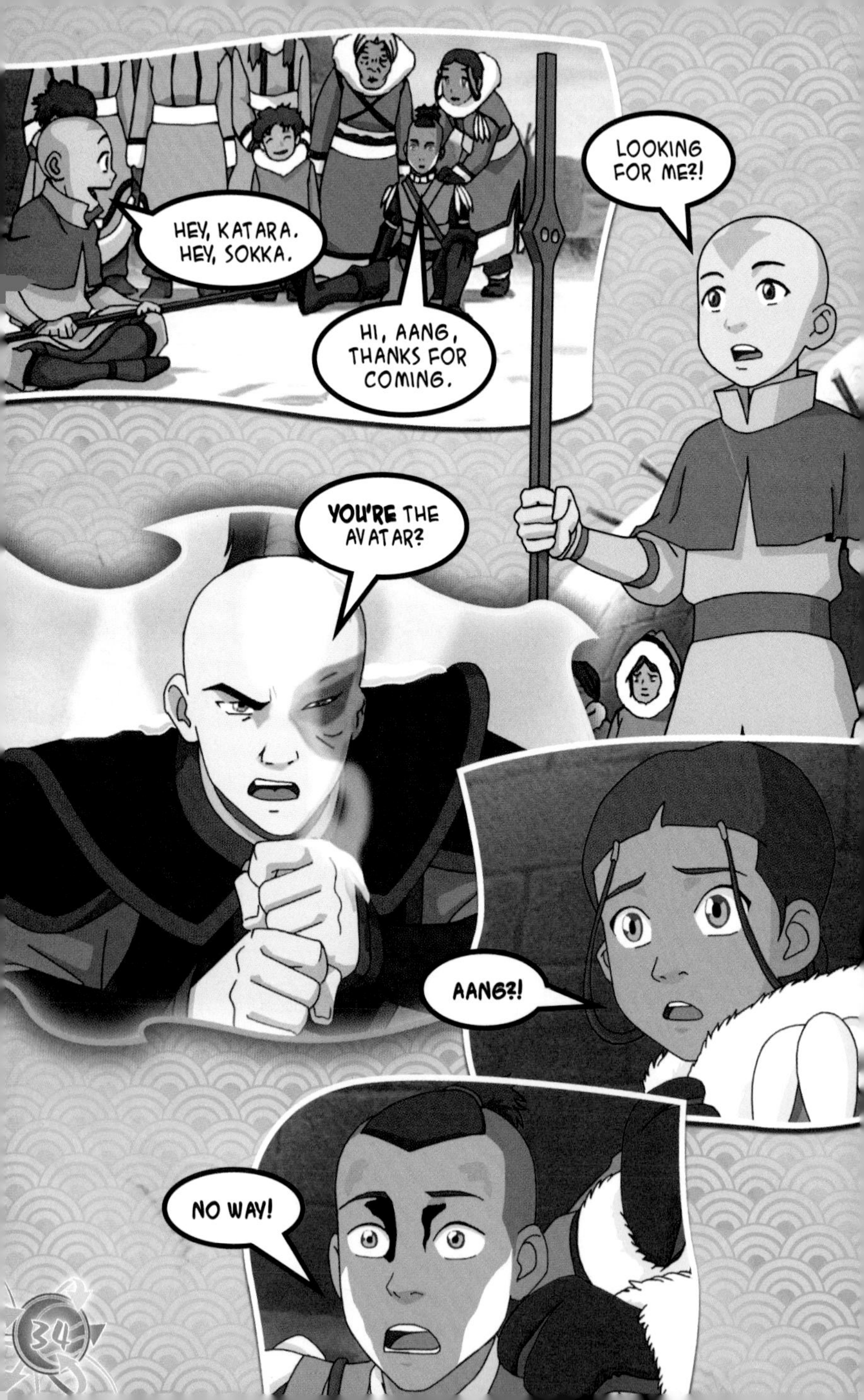
HEY, KATARA. HEY, SOKKA.
HI, AANG, THANKS FOR COMING.
LOOKING FOR ME?!
YOU'RE THE AVATAR?
AANG?!
NO WAY!

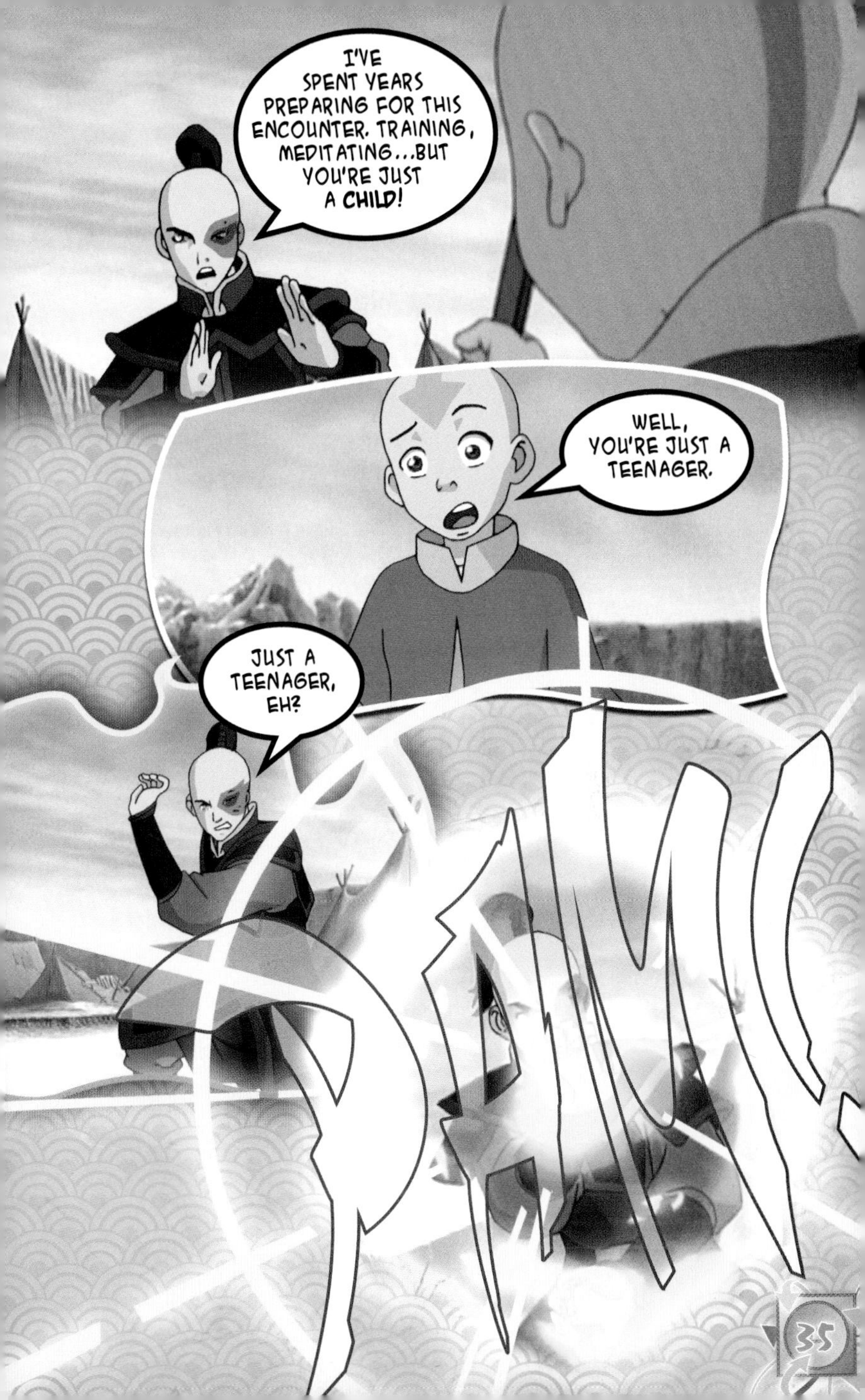
I'VE SPENT YEARS PREPARING FOR THIS ENCOUNTER. TRAINING, MEDITATING...BUT YOU'RE JUST A CHILD!
WELL, YOU'RE JUST A TEENAGER.
JUST A TEENAGER, EH?

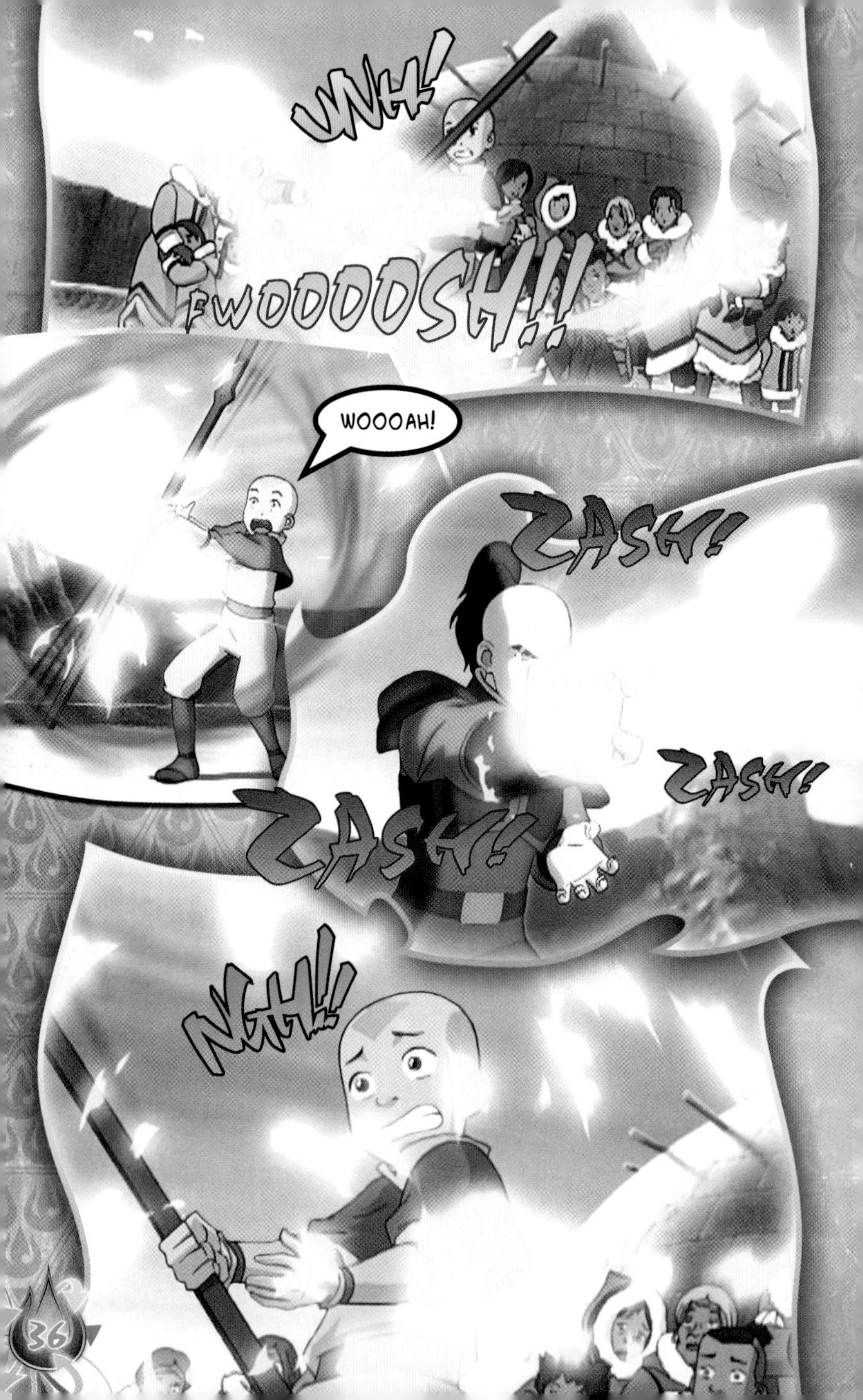
UNH!
FWOOOOSH!!
WOOOAH!
ZASH!
ZASH!
ZASH!
NGH!!

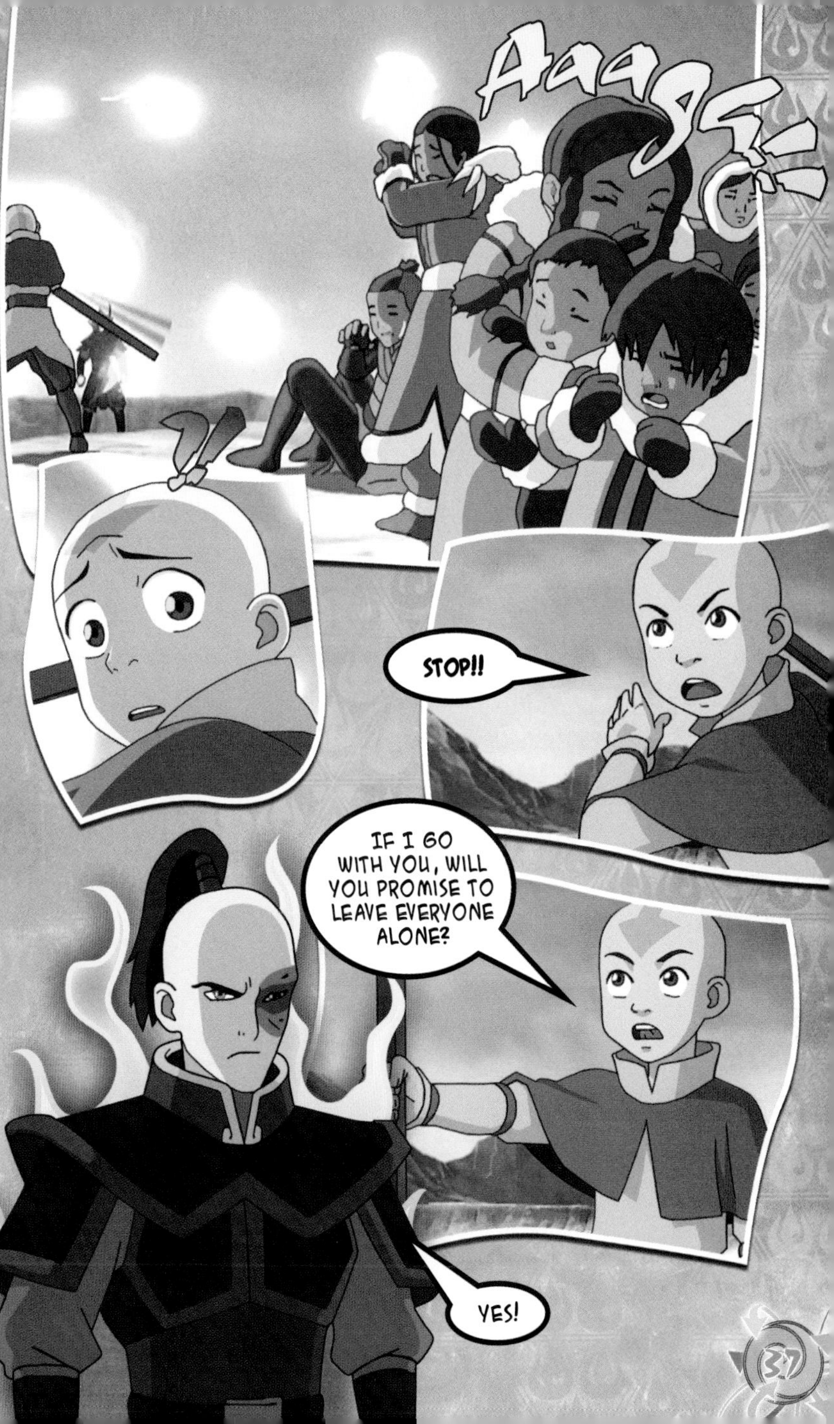
Aaagh!!
STOP!!
IF I GO WITH YOU, WILL YOU PROMISE TO LEAVE EVERYONE ALONE?
YES!

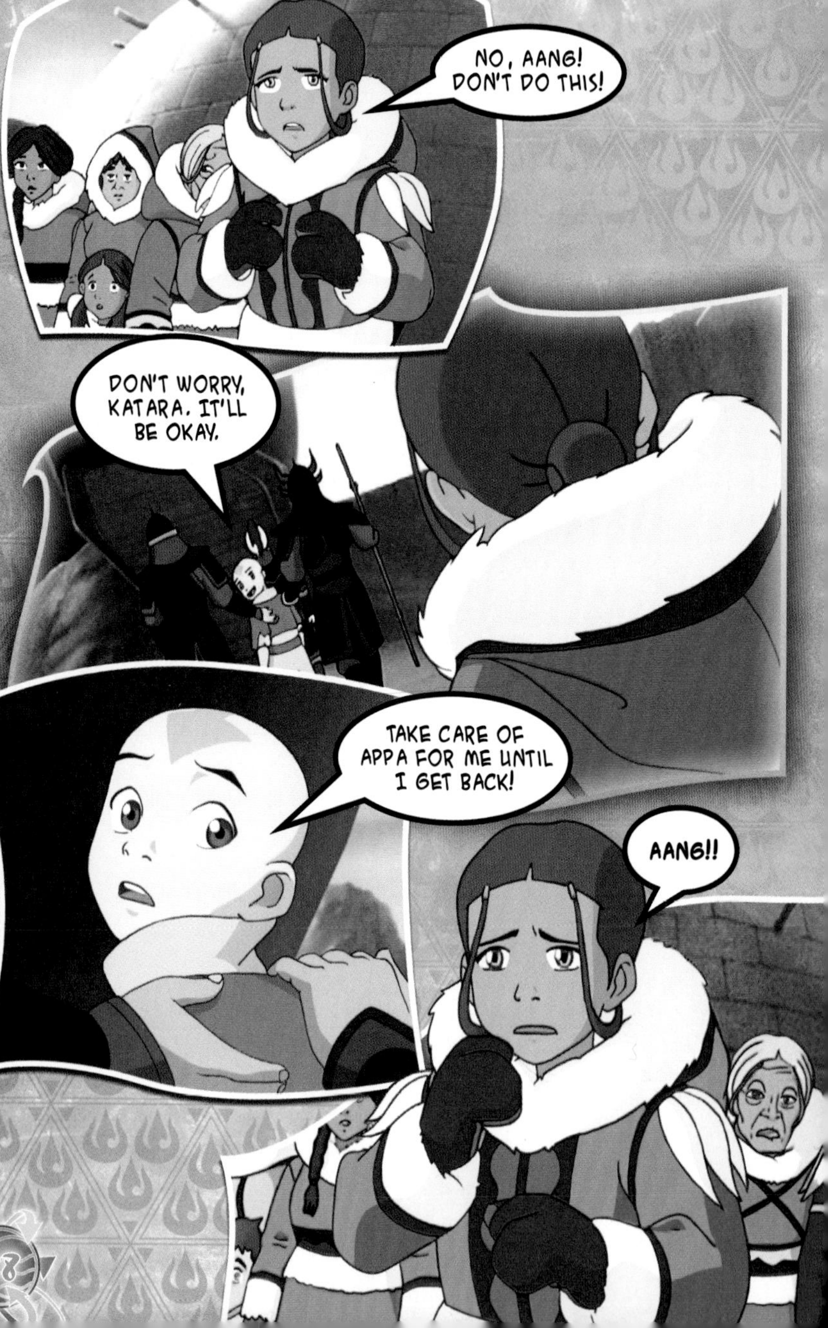
NO, AANG! DON'T DO THIS!
DON'T WORRY, KATARA. IT'LL BE OKAY.
TAKE CARE OF APPA FOR ME UNTIL I GET BACK!
AANG!!

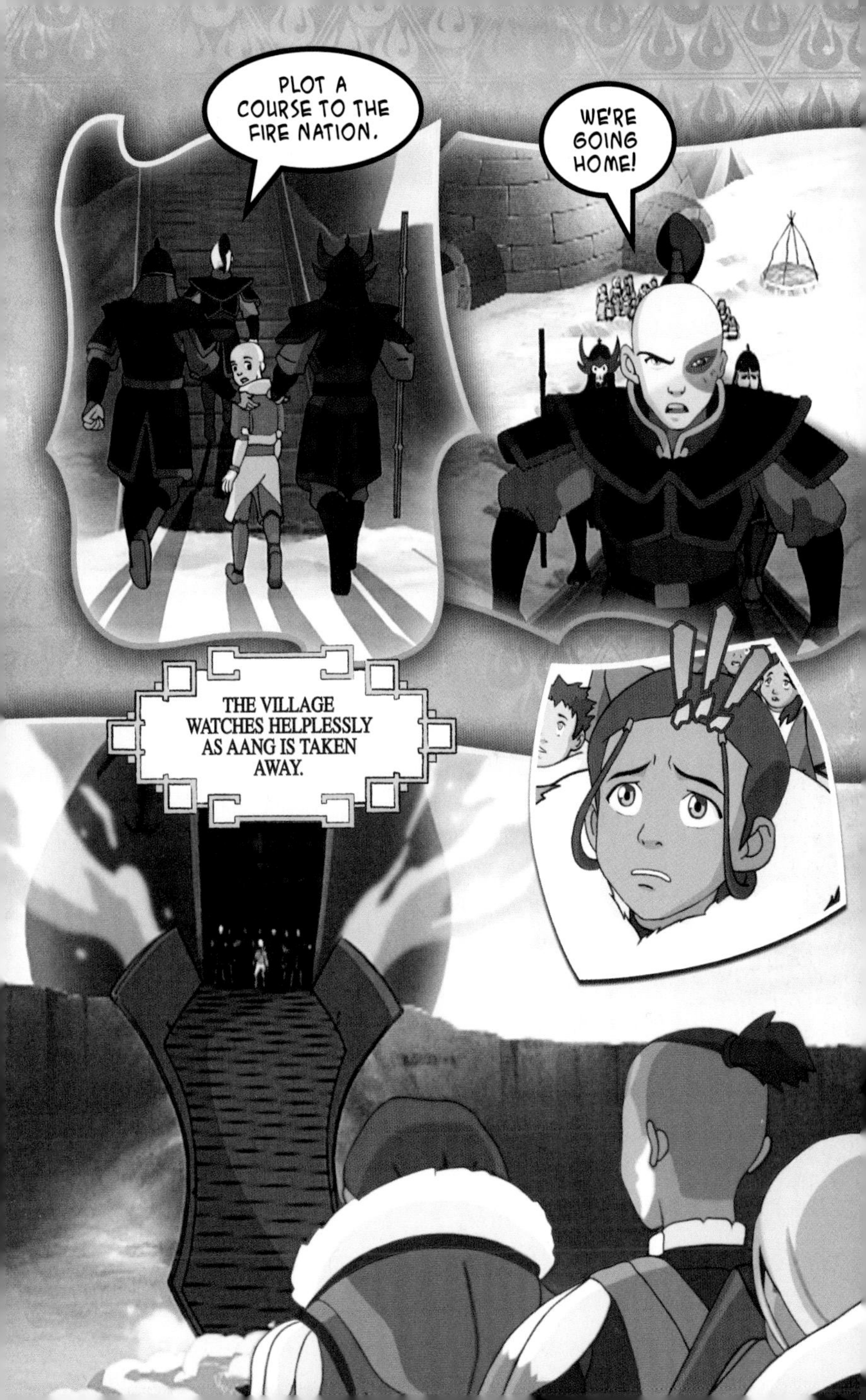
PLOT A COURSE TO THE FIRE NATION.
WE'RE GOING HOME!
THE VILLAGE WATCHES HELPLESSLY AS AANG IS TAKEN AWAY.

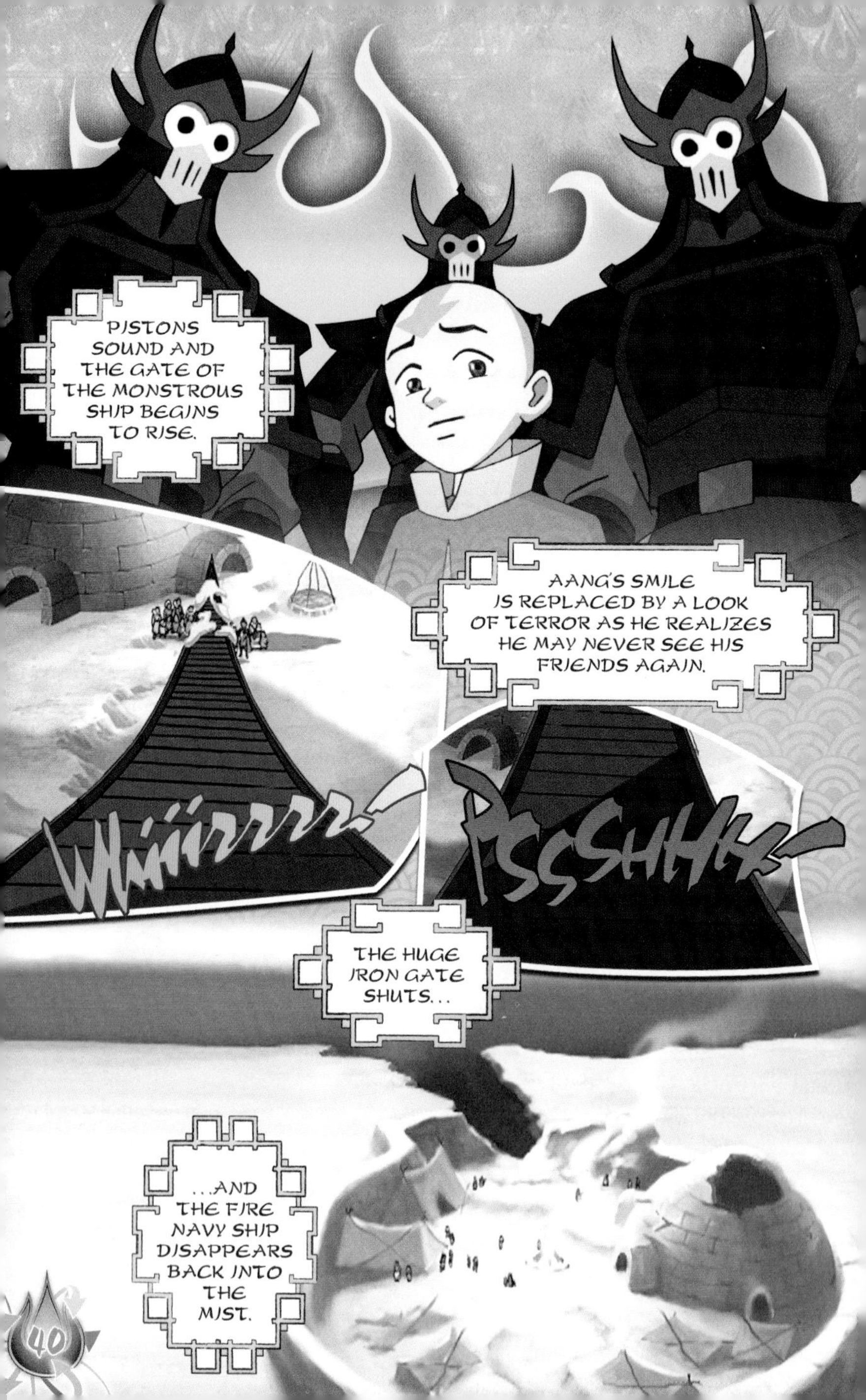
PISTONS SOUND AND THE GATE OF THE MONSTROUS SHIP BEGINS TO RISE.
AANG'S SMILE IS REPLACED BY A LOOK OF TERROR AS HE REALIZES HE MAY NEVER SEE HIS FRIENDS AGAIN.
WHiiirrrr!
PSSSHHH!
THE HUGE IRON GATE SHUTS...
...AND THE FIRE NAVY SHIP DISAPPEARS BACK INTO THE MIST.

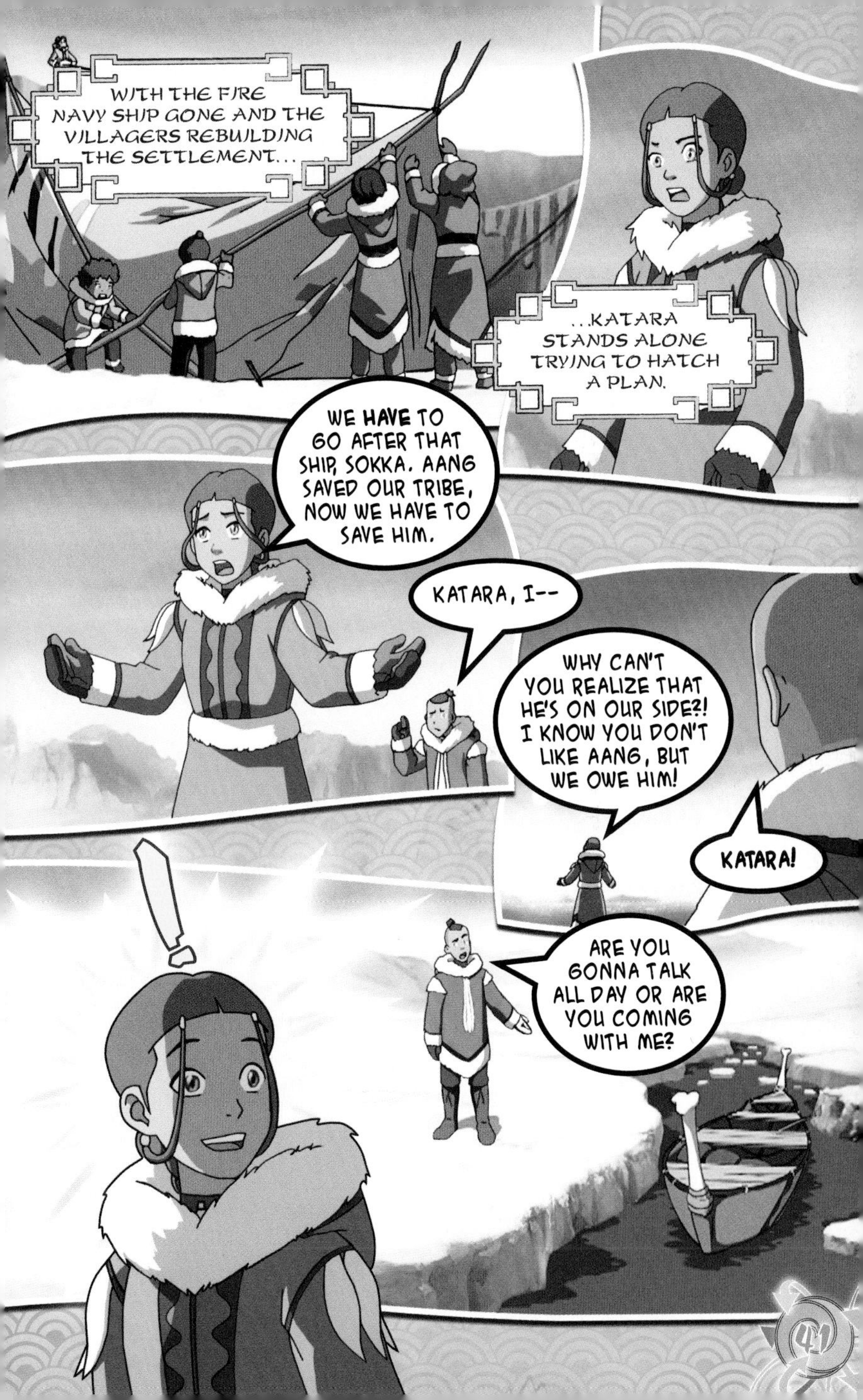
WITH THE FIRE NAVY SHIP GONE AND THE VILLAGERS REBUILDING THE SETTLEMENT...
...KATARA STANDS ALONE TRYING TO HATCH A PLAN.
WE HAVE TO GO AFTER THAT SHIP, SOKKA. AANG SAVED OUR TRIBE, NOW WE HAVE TO SAVE HIM.
KATARA, I--
WHY CAN'T YOU REALIZE THAT HE'S ON OUR SIDE?! I KNOW YOU DON'T LIKE AANG, BUT WE OWE HIM!
KATARA!
!
ARE YOU GONNA TALK ALL DAY OR ARE YOU COMING WITH ME?

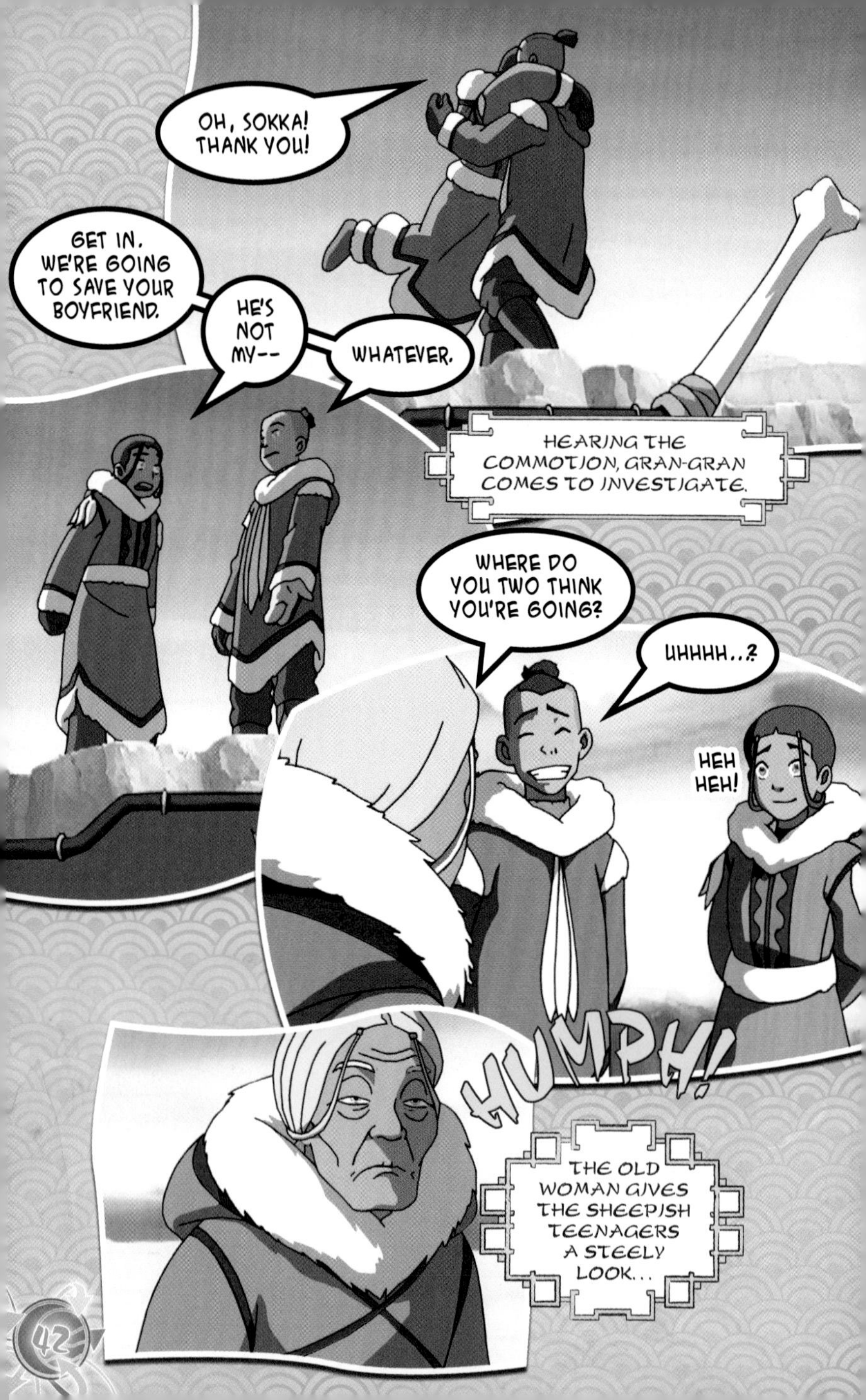
OH, SOKKA! THANK YOU!
GET IN. WE'RE GOING TO SAVE YOUR BOYFRIEND.
HE'S NOT MY--
WHATEVER.
HEARING THE COMMOTION, GRAN-GRAN COMES TO INVESTIGATE.
WHERE DO YOU TWO THINK YOU'RE GOING?
UHHHH...?
HEH HEH!
HUMPH!
THE OLD WOMAN GIVES THE SHEEPISH TEENAGERS A STEELY LOOK...

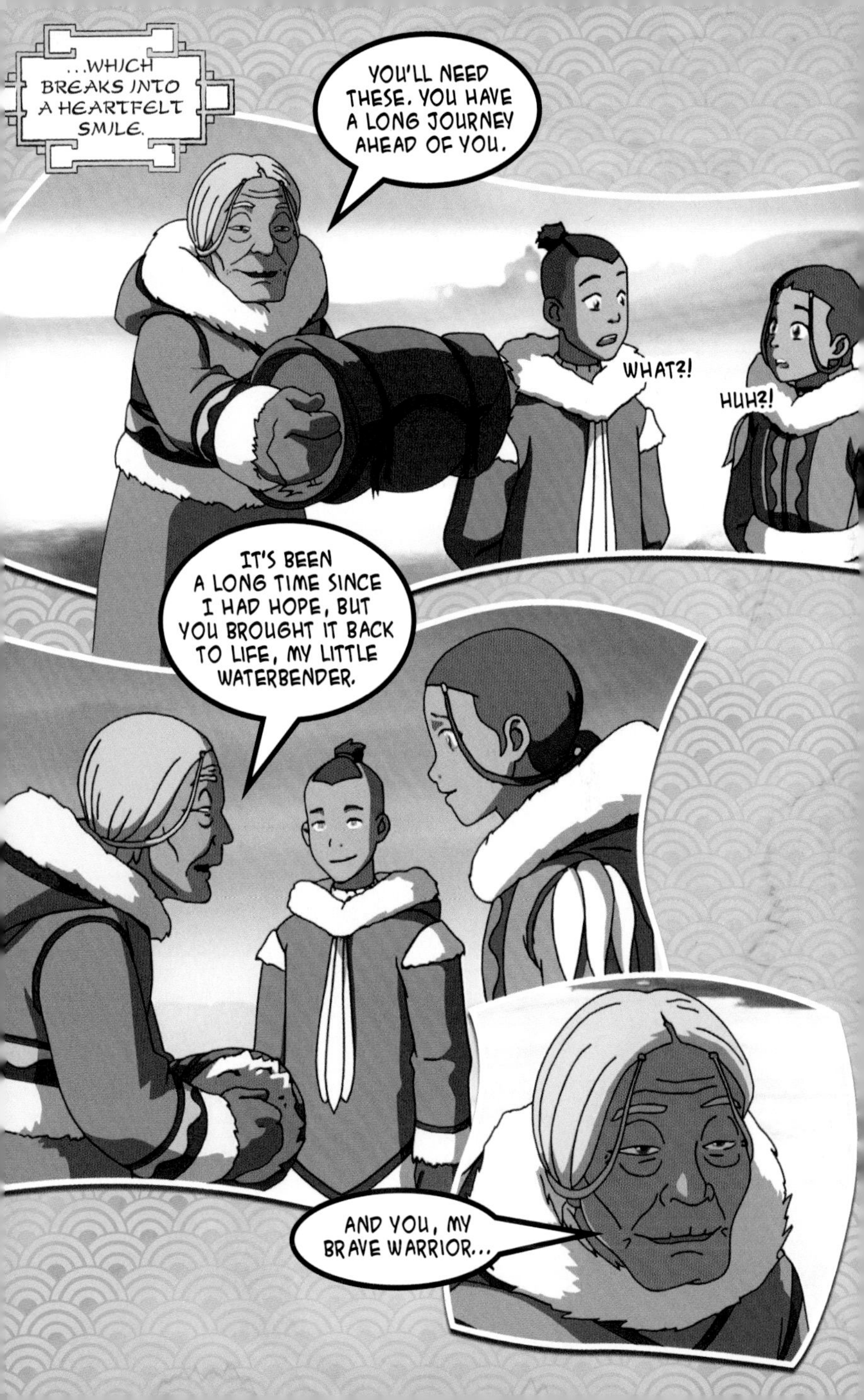
...WHICH BREAKS INTO A HEARTFELT SMILE.
YOU'LL NEED THESE. YOU HAVE A LONG JOURNEY AHEAD OF YOU.
WHAT?!
HUH?!
IT'S BEEN A LONG TIME SINCE I HAD HOPE, BUT YOU BROUGHT IT BACK TO LIFE, MY LITTLE WATERBENDER.
AND YOU, MY BRAVE WARRIOR...

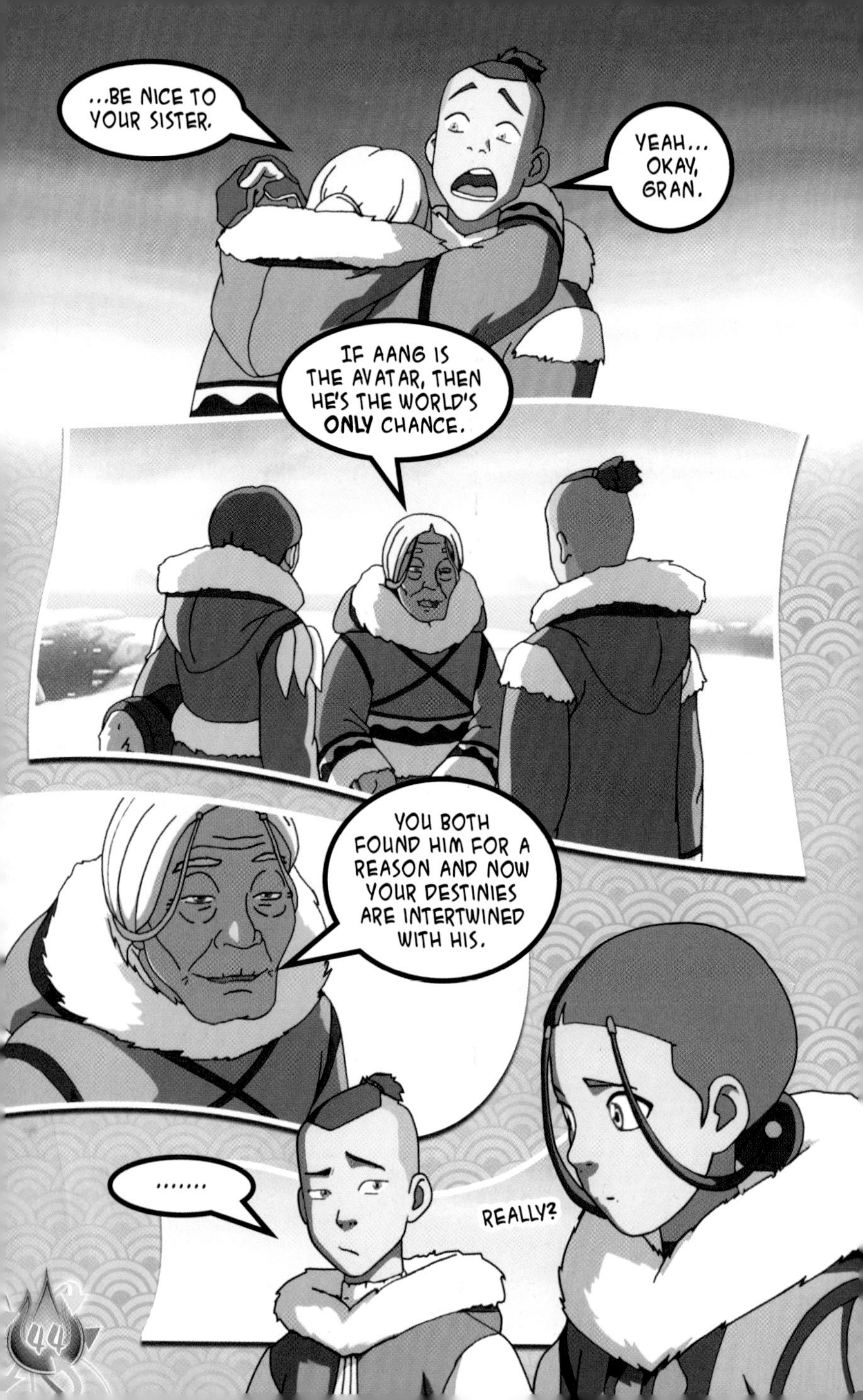
...BE NICE TO YOUR SISTER.
YEAH... OKAY, GRAN.
IF AANG IS THE AVATAR, THEN HE'S THE WORLD'S **ONLY** CHANCE.
YOU BOTH FOUND HIM FOR A REASON AND NOW YOUR DESTINIES ARE INTERTWINED WITH HIS.
....
REALLY?

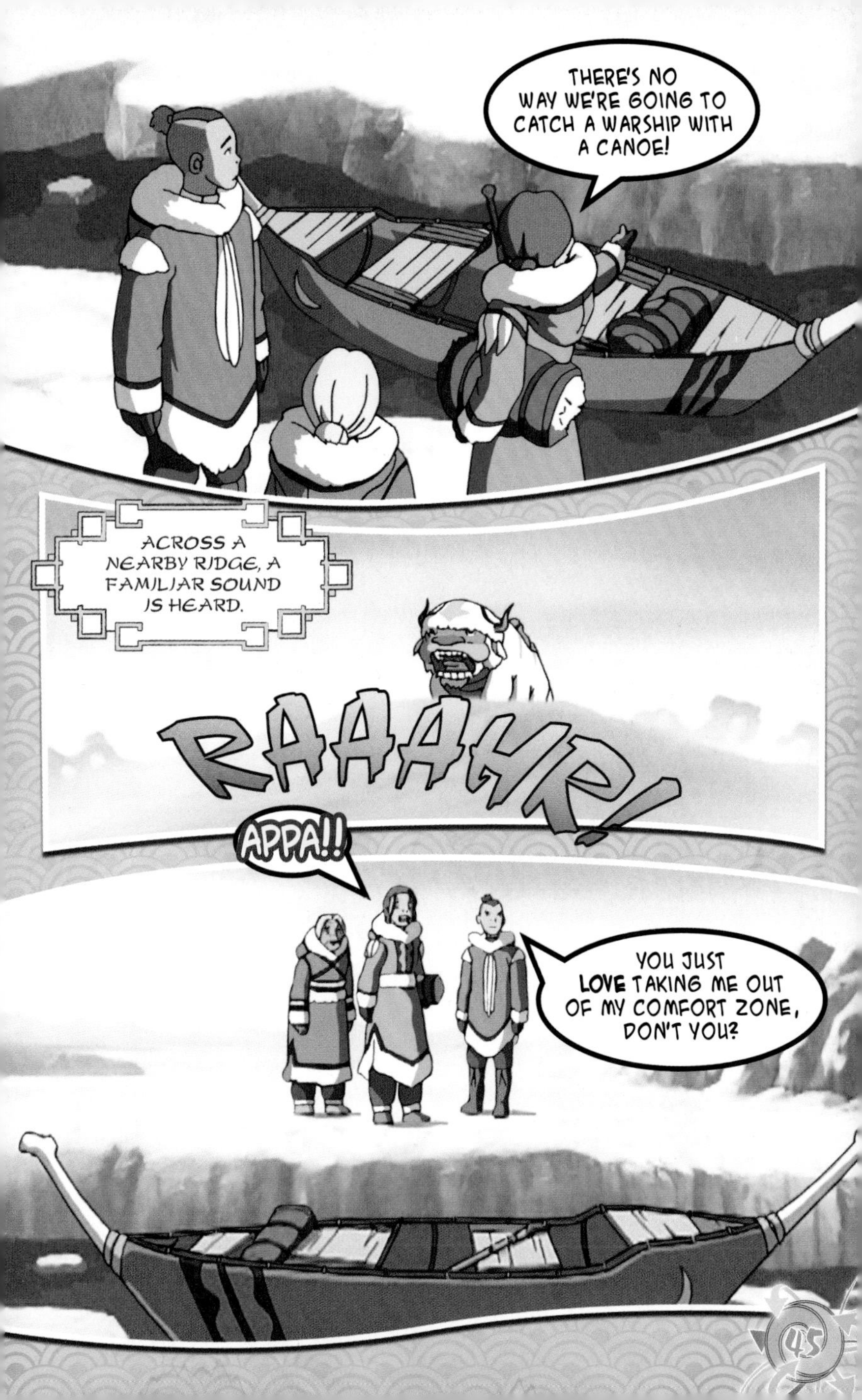
THERE'S NO WAY WE'RE GOING TO CATCH A WARSHIP WITH A CANOE!
ACROSS A NEARBY RIDGE, A FAMILIAR SOUND IS HEARD.
RAAAHR!
APPA!!
YOU JUST **LOVE** TAKING ME OUT OF MY COMFORT ZONE, DON'T YOU?

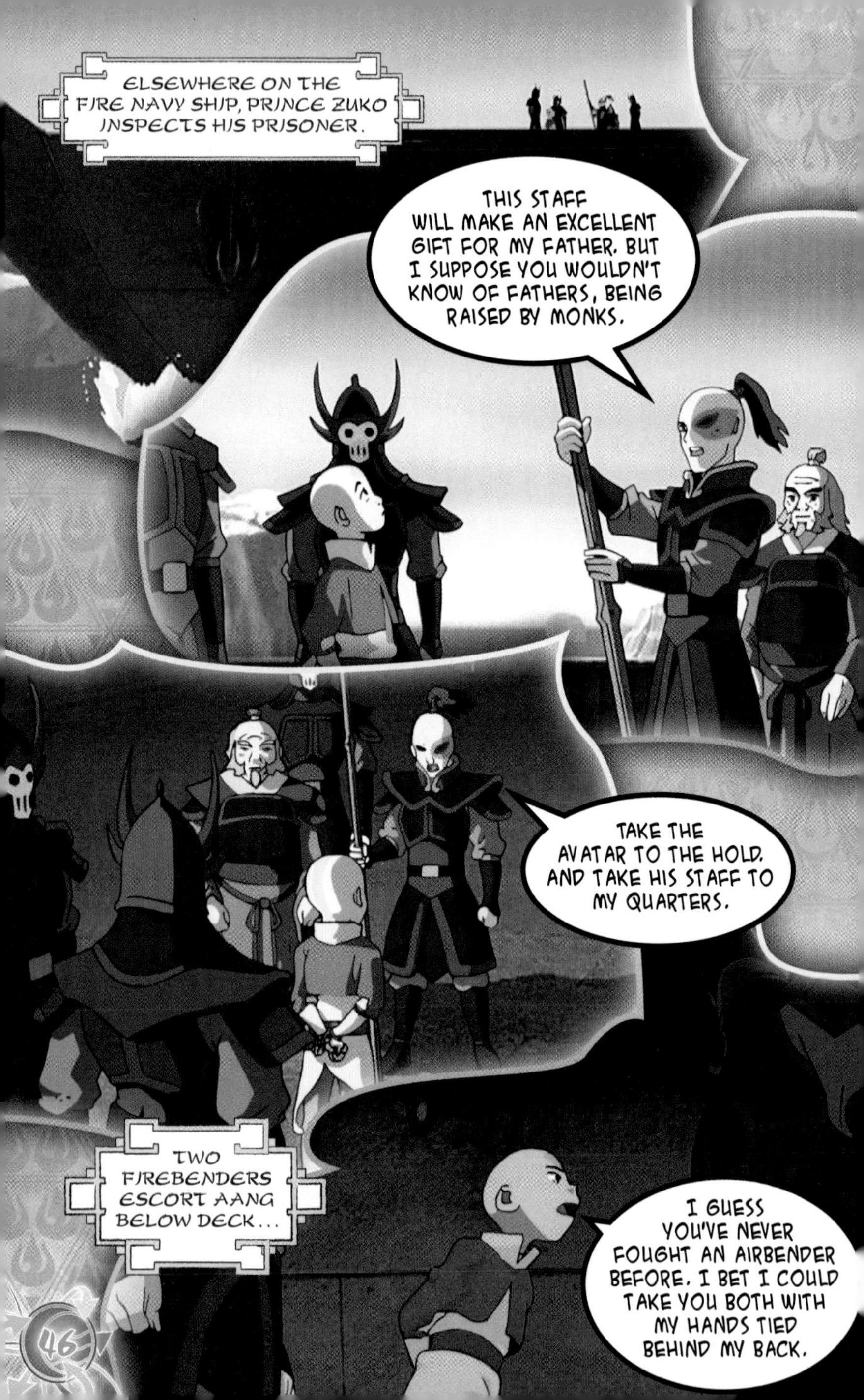
ELSEWHERE ON THE FIRE NAVY SHIP, PRINCE ZUKO INSPECTS HIS PRISONER.
THIS STAFF WILL MAKE AN EXCELLENT GIFT FOR MY FATHER. BUT I SUPPOSE YOU WOULDN'T KNOW OF FATHERS, BEING RAISED BY MONKS.
TAKE THE AVATAR TO THE HOLD. AND TAKE HIS STAFF TO MY QUARTERS.
TWO FIREBENDERS ESCORT AANG BELOW DECK...
I GUESS YOU'VE NEVER FOUGHT AN AIRBENDER BEFORE. I BET I COULD TAKE YOU BOTH WITH MY HANDS TIED BEHIND MY BACK.

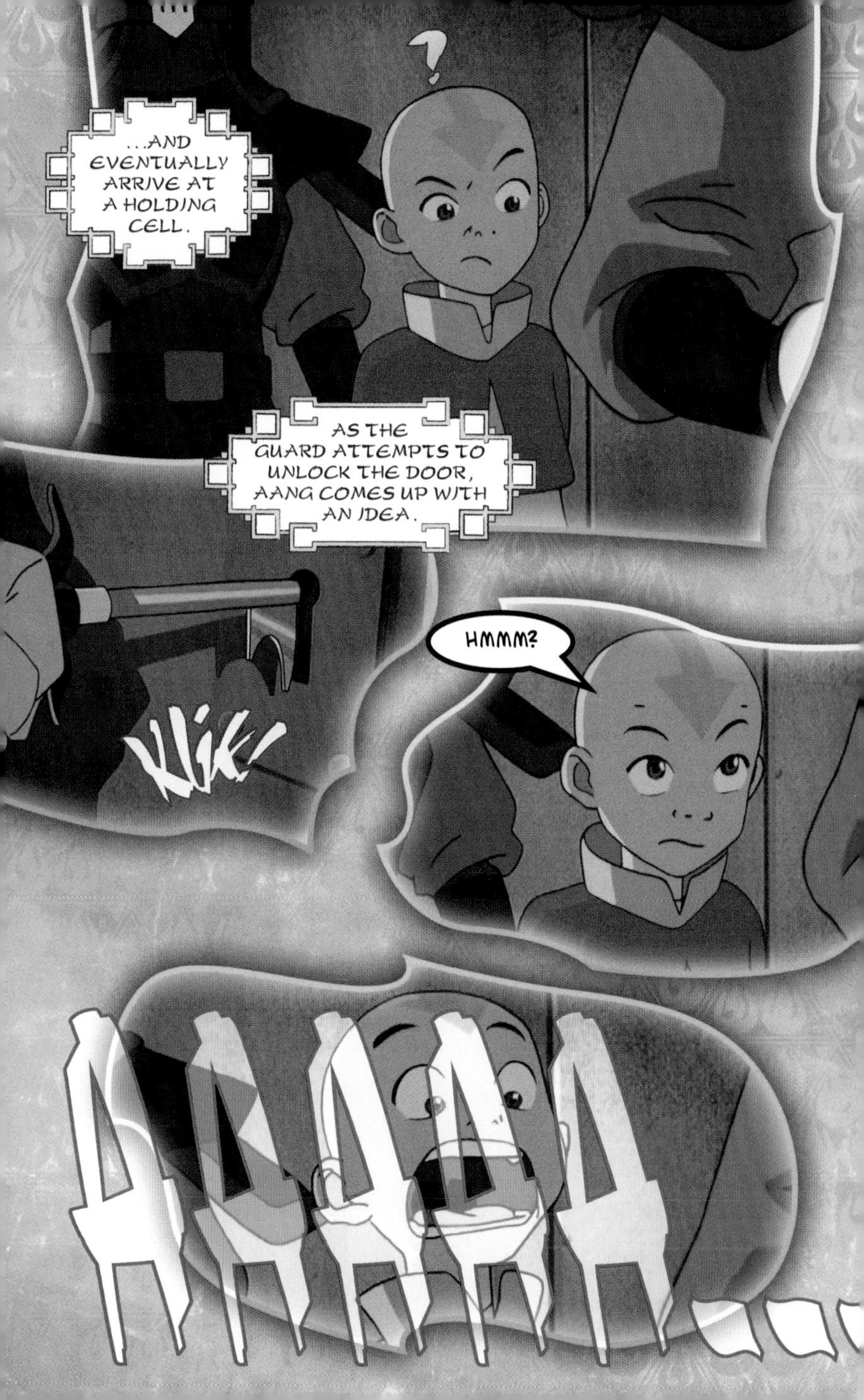
...AND EVENTUALLY ARRIVE AT A HOLDING CELL.
AS THE GUARD ATTEMPTS TO UNLOCK THE DOOR, AANG COMES UP WITH AN IDEA.
KLIK!
HMMM?
AAAAA....

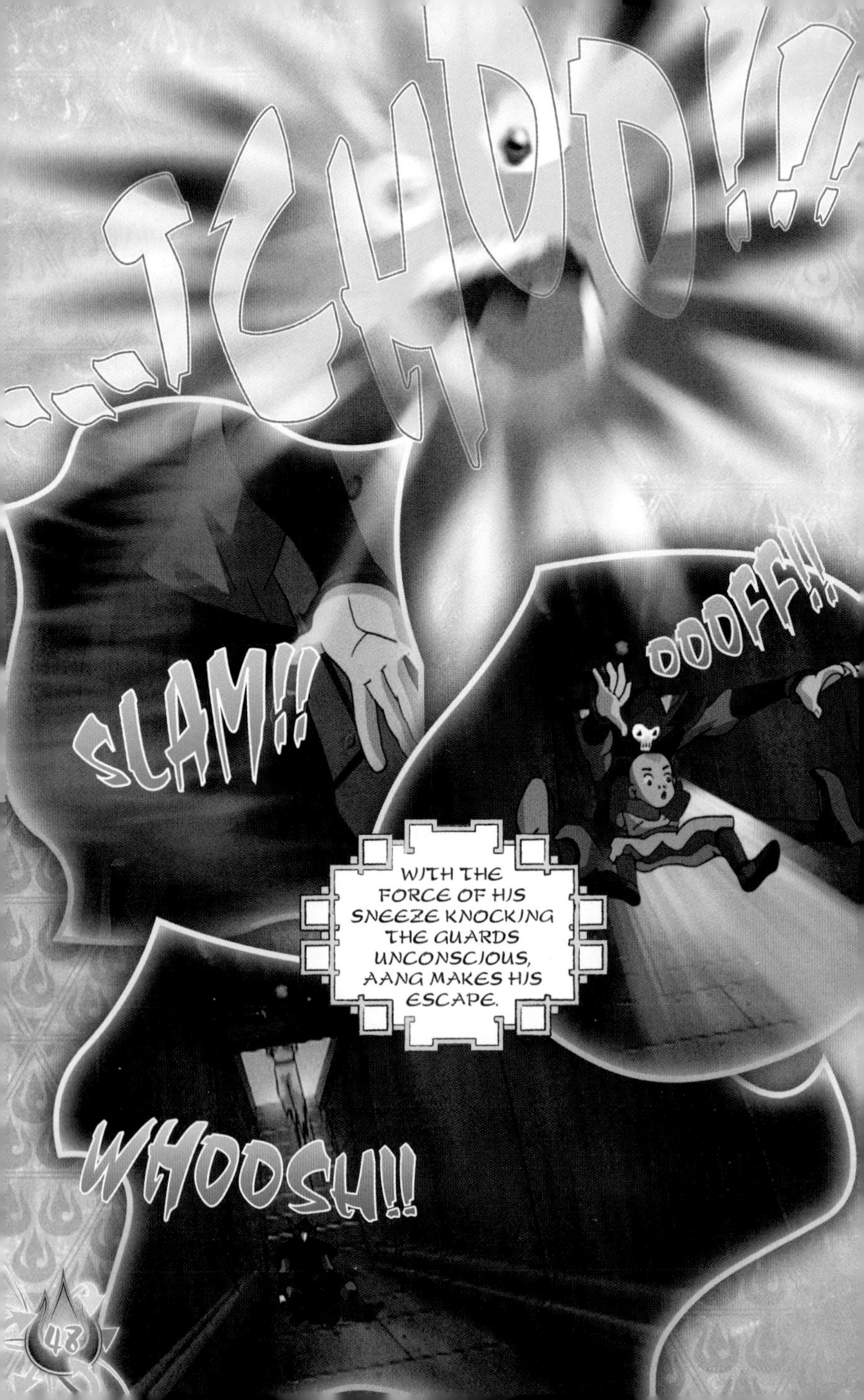
...TCHOO!!!
SLAM!!
OOOFF!!
WITH THE FORCE OF HIS SNEEZE KNOCKING THE GUARDS UNCONSCIOUS, AANG MAKES HIS ESCAPE.
WHOOSH!!

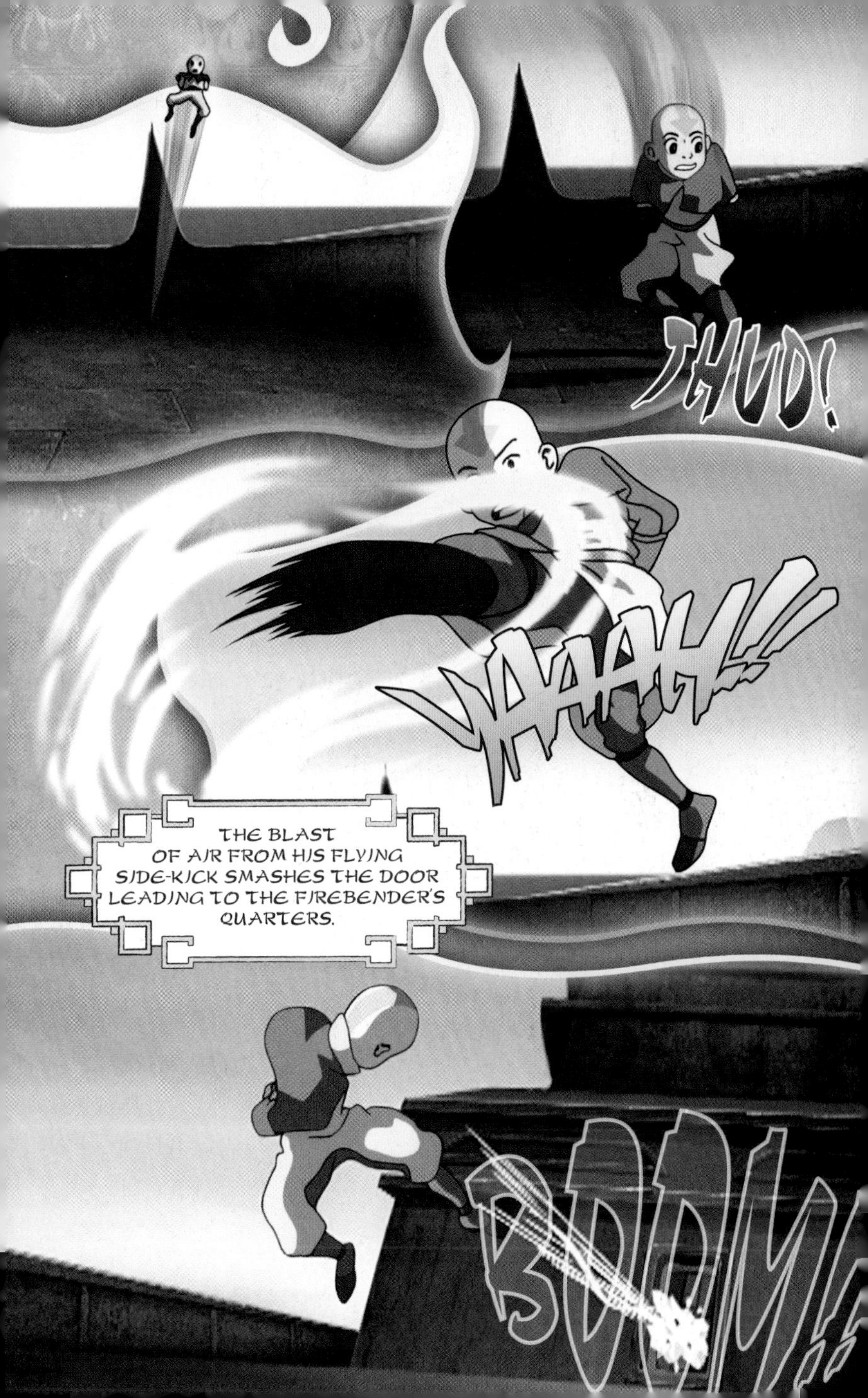
THUD!
YAAAH!!
THE BLAST OF AIR FROM HIS FLYING SIDE-KICK SMASHES THE DOOR LEADING TO THE FIREBENDER'S QUARTERS.
BOOM!

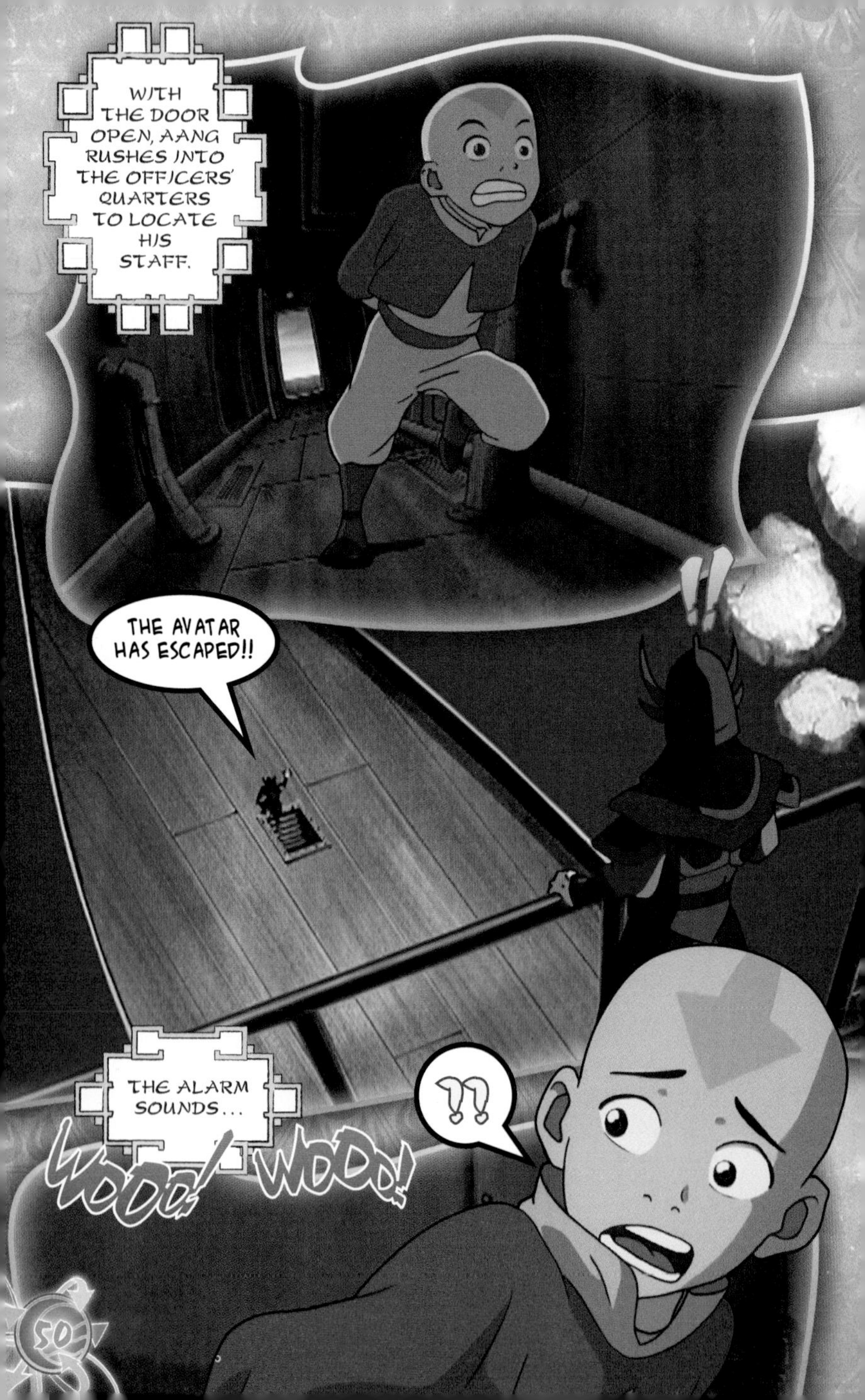
WITH THE DOOR OPEN, AANG RUSHES INTO THE OFFICERS' QUARTERS TO LOCATE HIS STAFF.
THE AVATAR HAS ESCAPED!!
THE ALARM SOUNDS...
WOOO! WOOO!
??

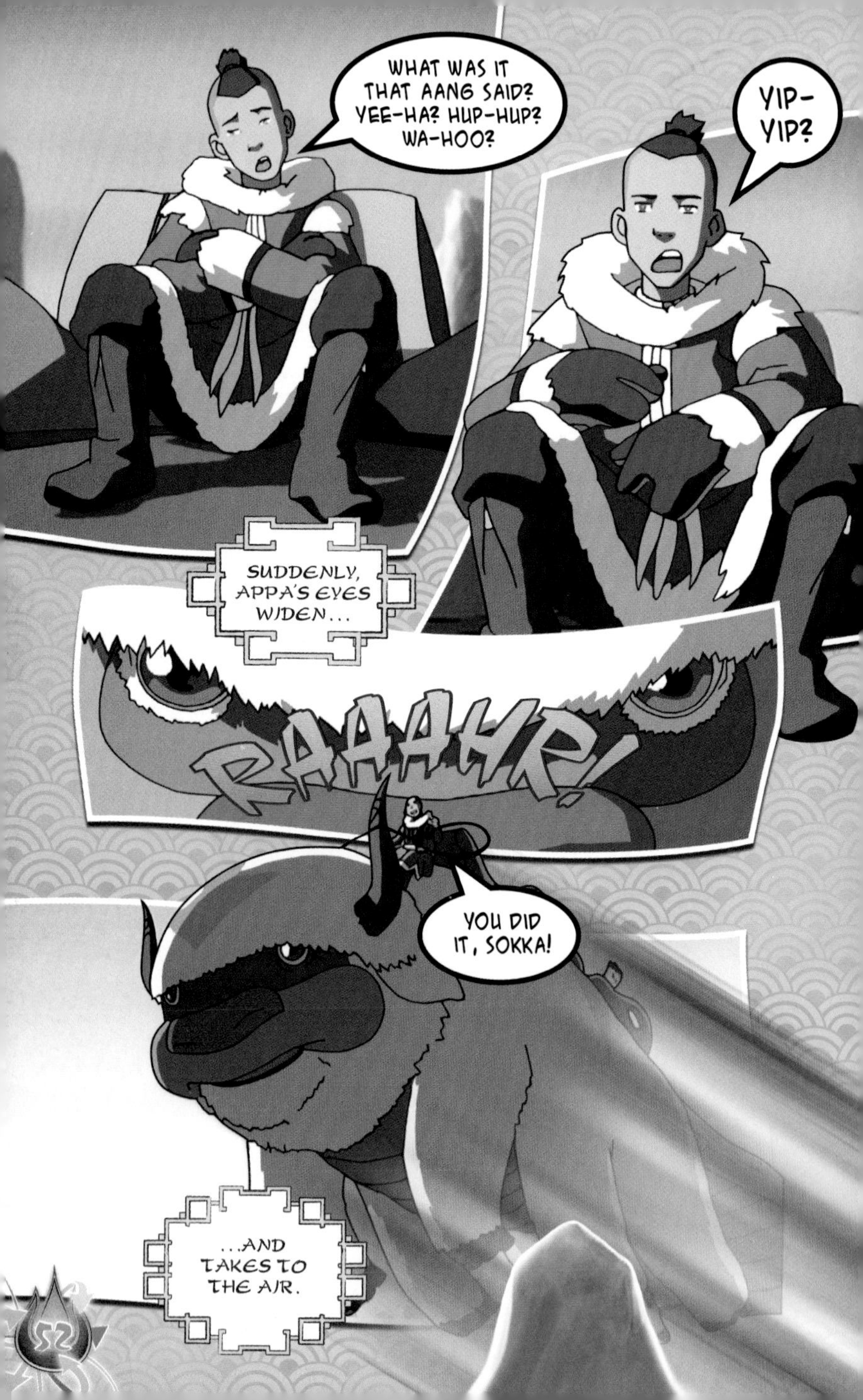
WHAT WAS IT THAT AANG SAID? YEE-HA? HUP-HUP? WA-HOO?
YIP-YIP?
SUDDENLY, APPA'S EYES WIDEN...
RAAAHR!
YOU DID IT, SOKKA!
...AND TAKES TO THE AIR.

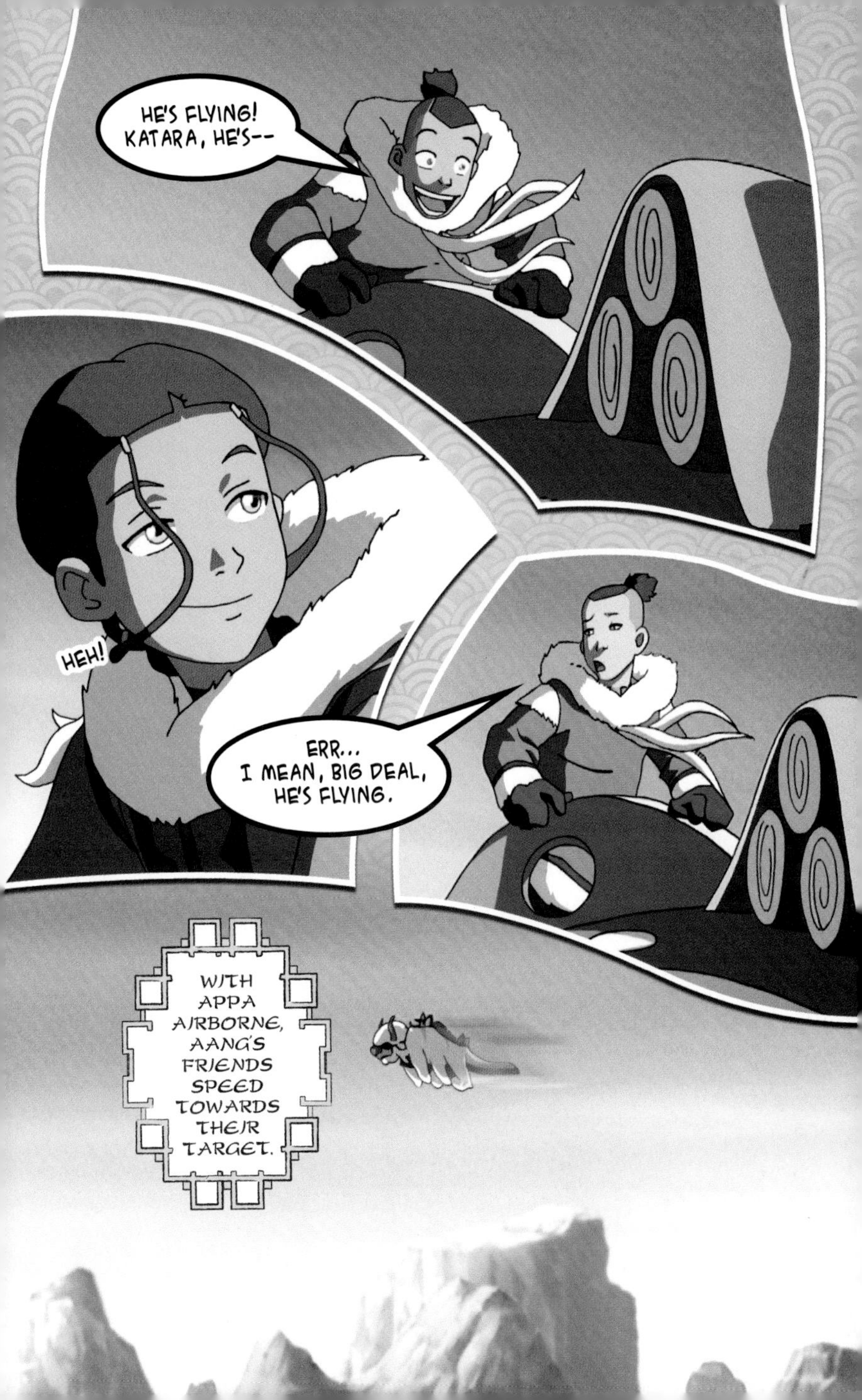
HE'S FLYING! KATARA, HE'S--
HEH!
ERR... I MEAN, BIG DEAL, HE'S FLYING.
WITH APPA AIRBORNE, AANG'S FRIENDS SPEED TOWARDS THEIR TARGET.

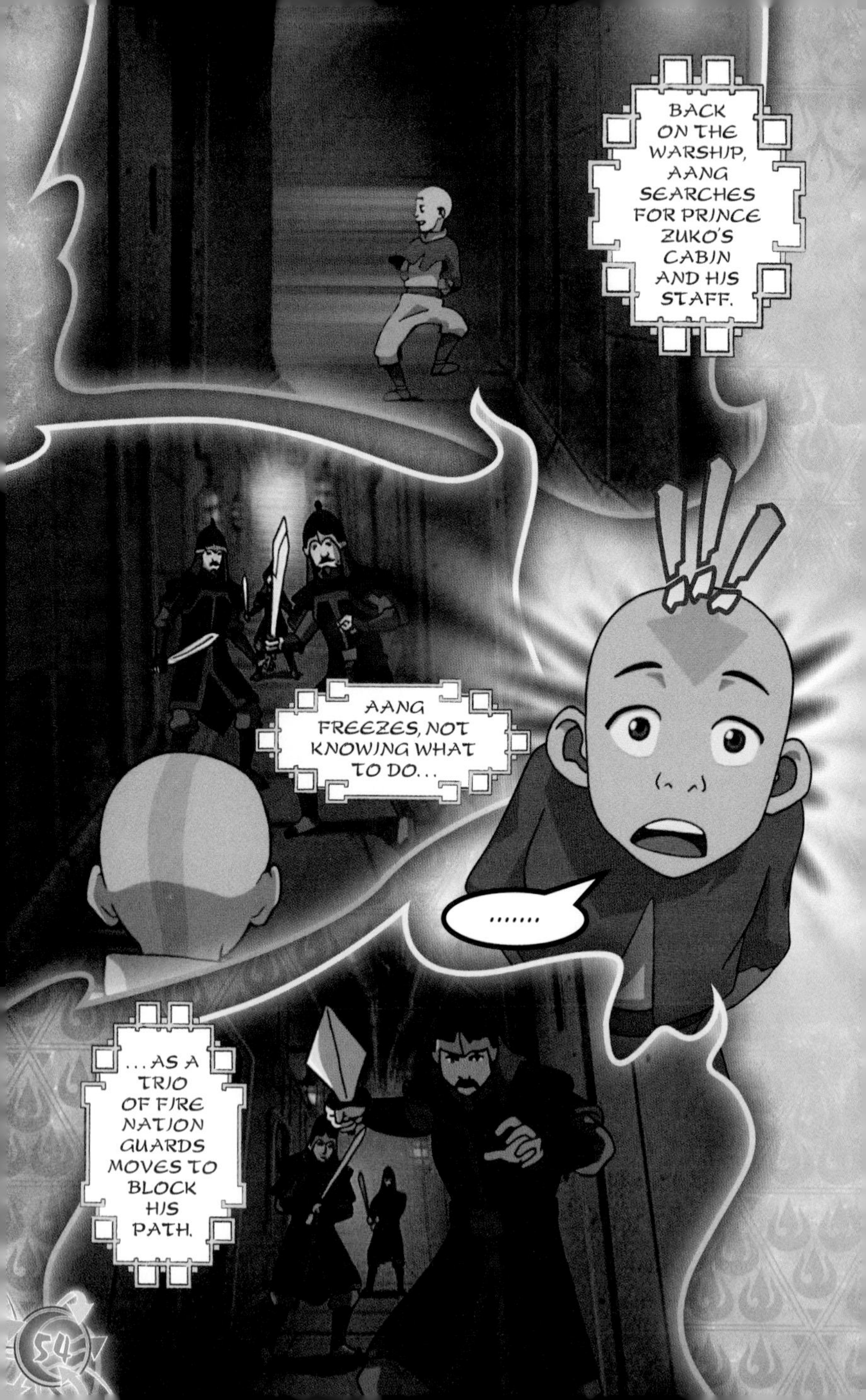
BACK ON THE WARSHIP, AANG SEARCHES FOR PRINCE ZUKO'S CABIN AND HIS STAFF.
AANG FREEZES, NOT KNOWING WHAT TO DO...
....
...AS A TRIO OF FIRE NATION GUARDS MOVES TO BLOCK HIS PATH.

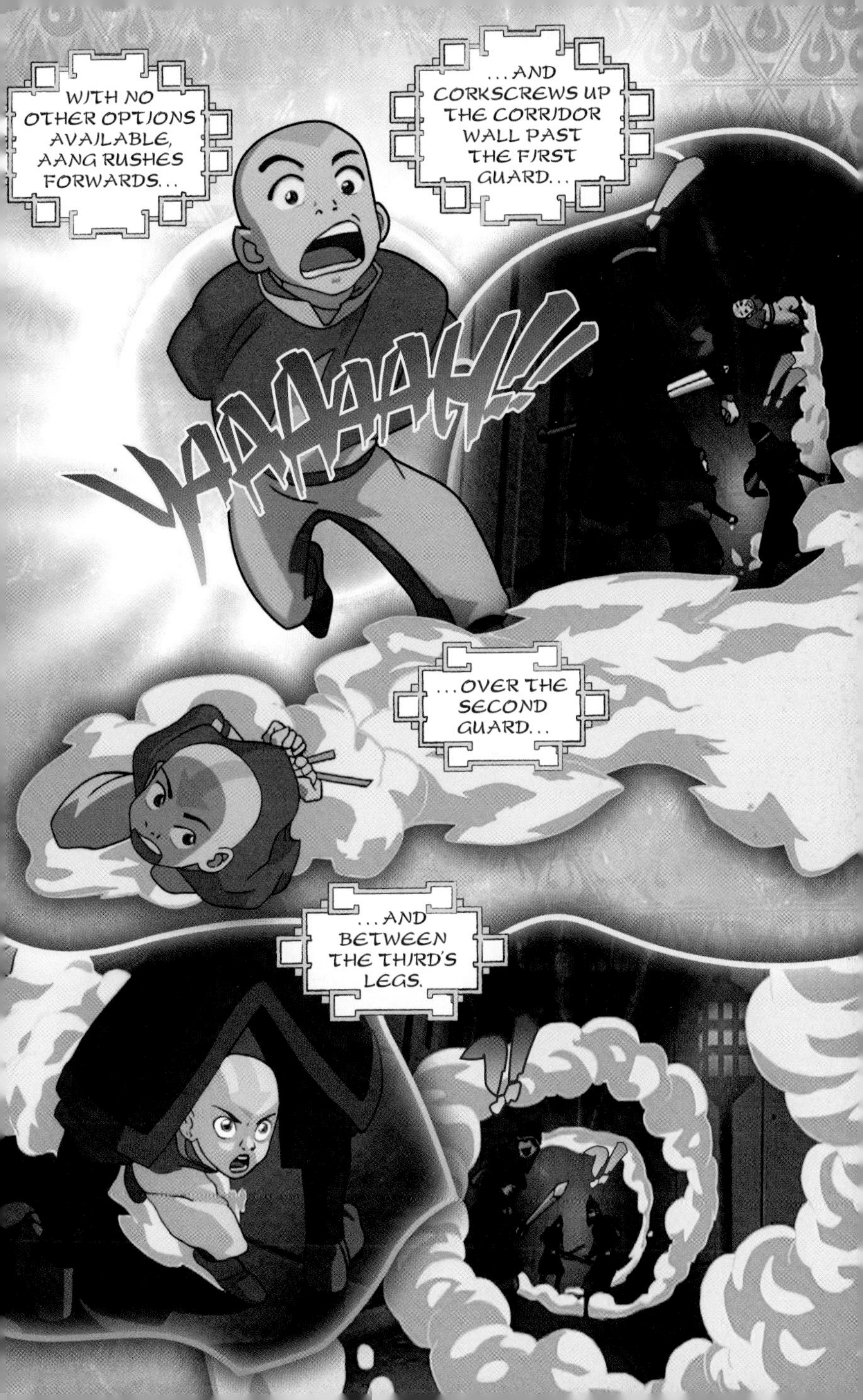
WITH NO OTHER OPTIONS AVAILABLE, AANG RUSHES FORWARDS...
...AND CORKSCREWS UP THE CORRIDOR WALL PAST THE FIRST GUARD...
YAAAAAH!!
...OVER THE SECOND GUARD...
...AND BETWEEN THE THIRD'S LEGS.

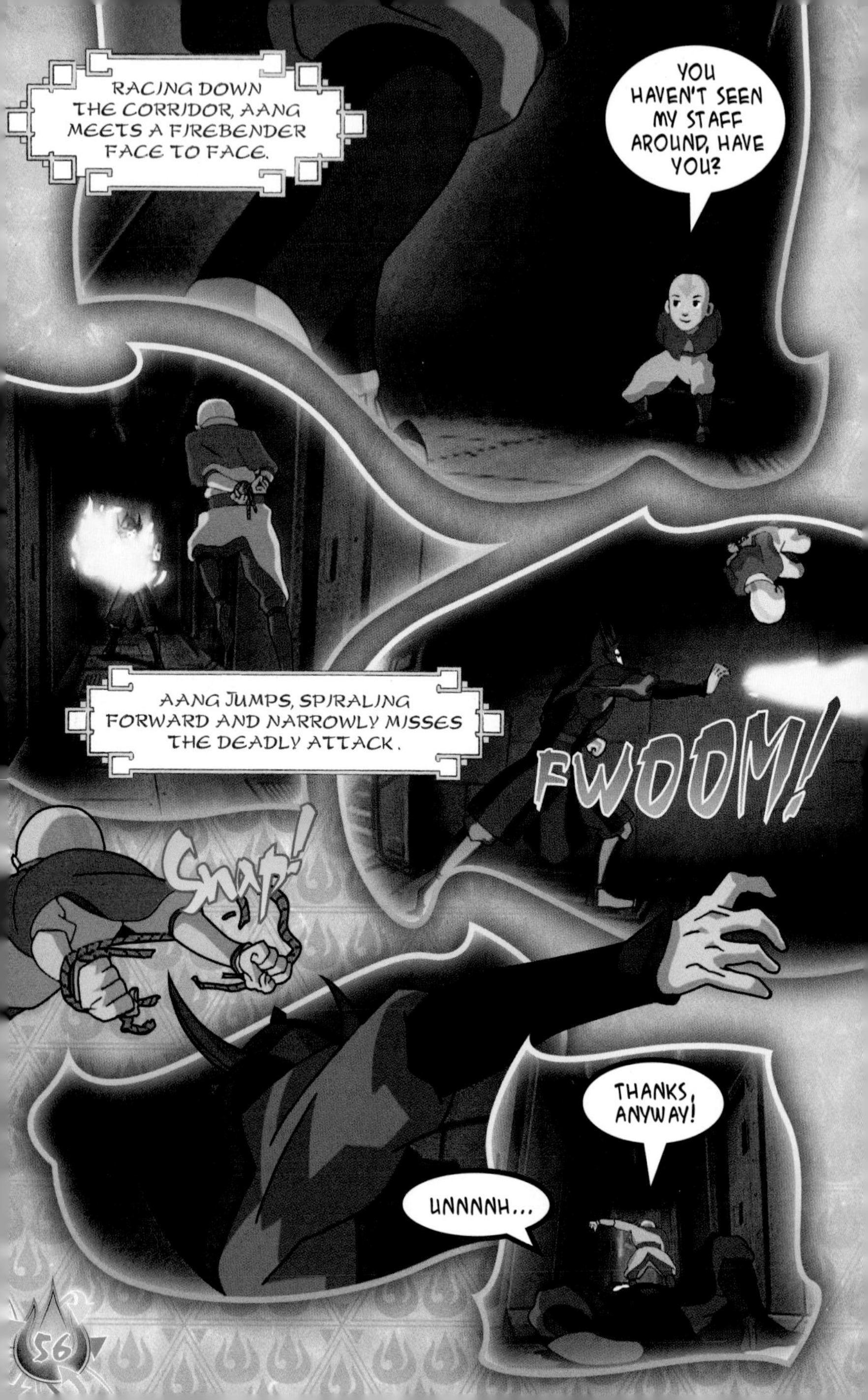
RACING DOWN THE CORRIDOR, AANG MEETS A FIREBENDER FACE TO FACE.
YOU HAVEN'T SEEN MY STAFF AROUND, HAVE YOU?
AANG JUMPS, SPIRALING FORWARD AND NARROWLY MISSES THE DEADLY ATTACK.
FWOOM!
SNAP!
THANKS, ANYWAY!
UNNNNH...

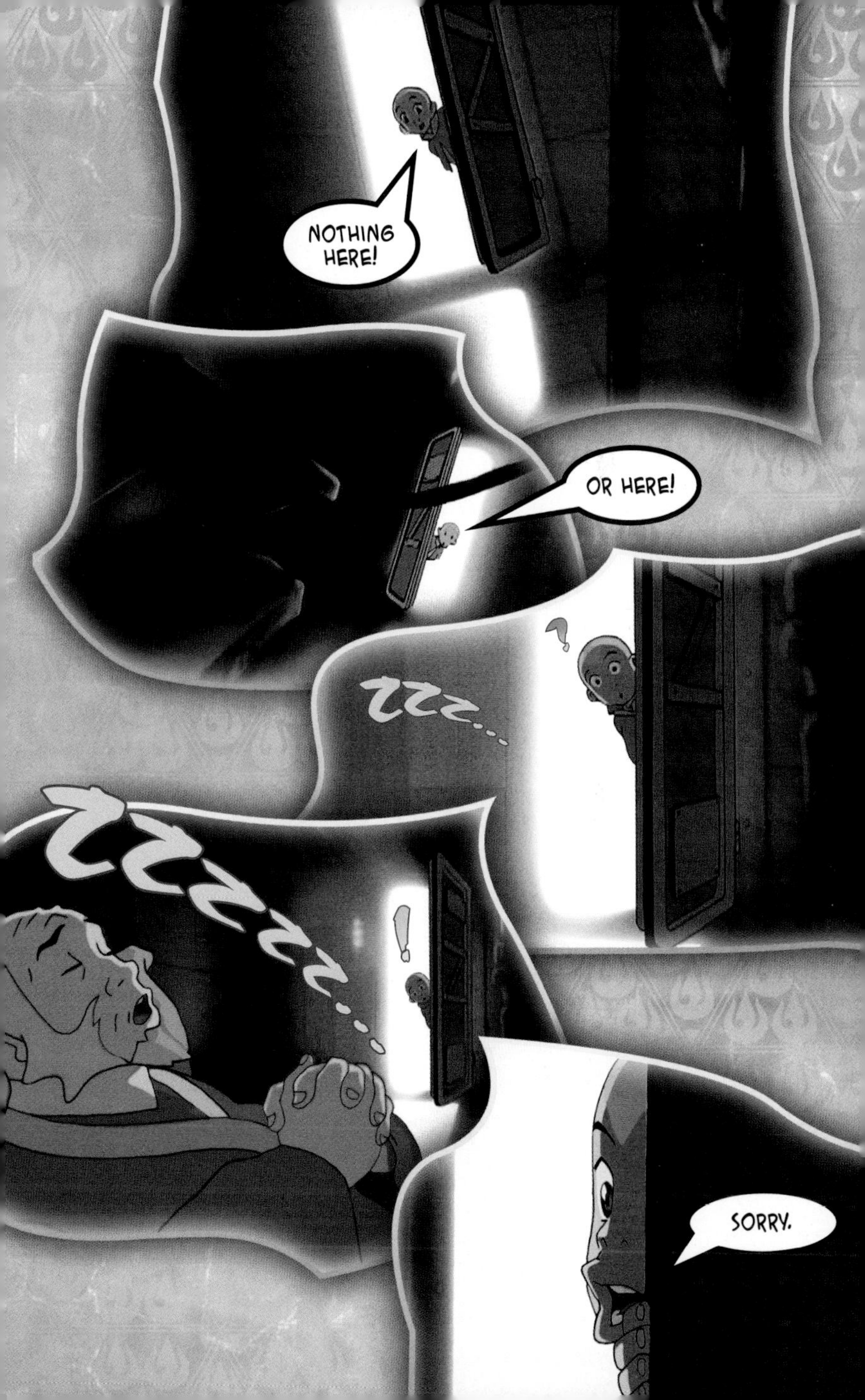
NOTHING HERE!
OR HERE!
ZZZ...
ZZZZZ....
SORRY.

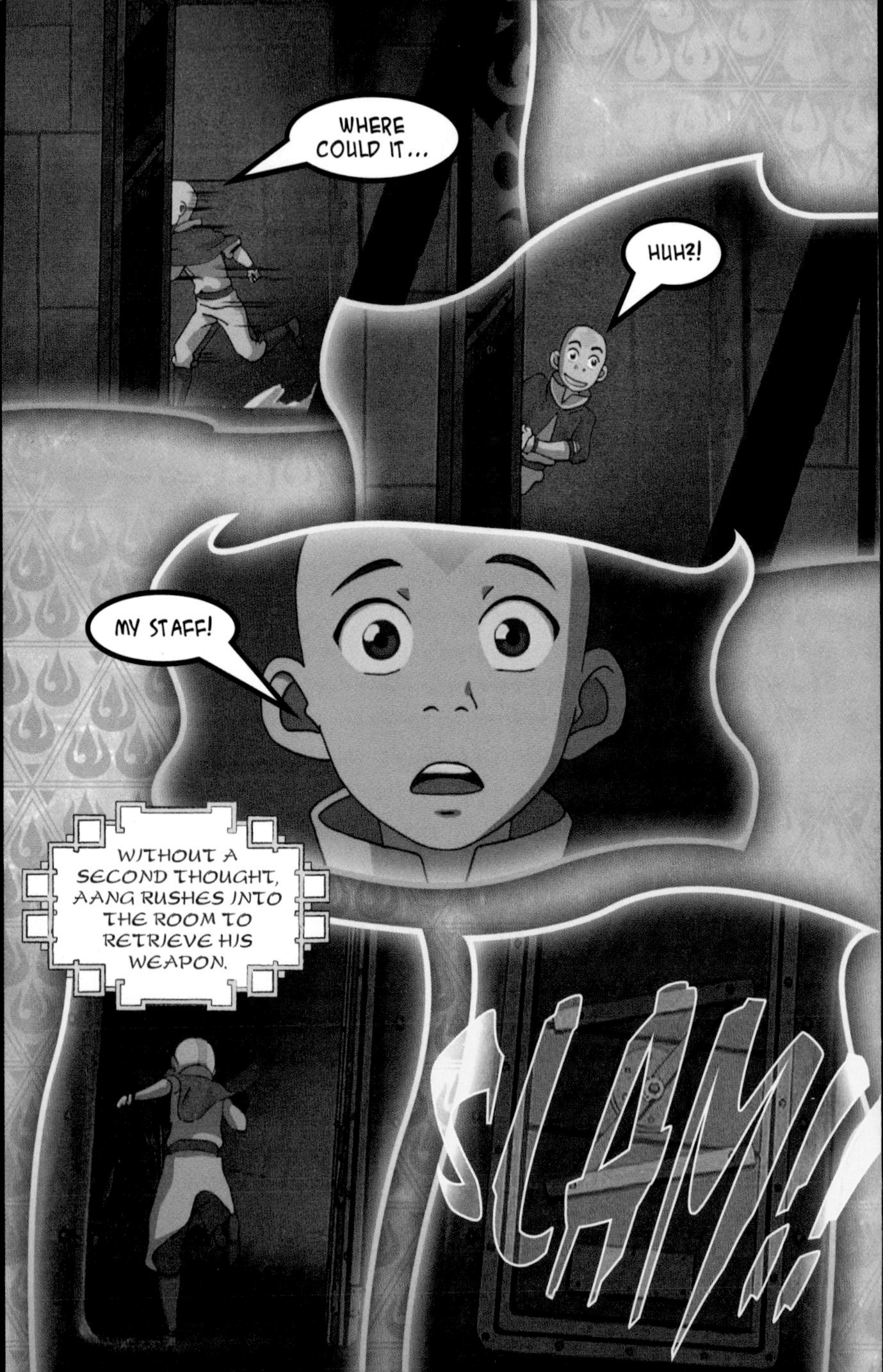
WHERE COULD IT...
HUH?!
MY STAFF!
WITHOUT A SECOND THOUGHT, AANG RUSHES INTO THE ROOM TO RETRIEVE HIS WEAPON.
SLAM!!

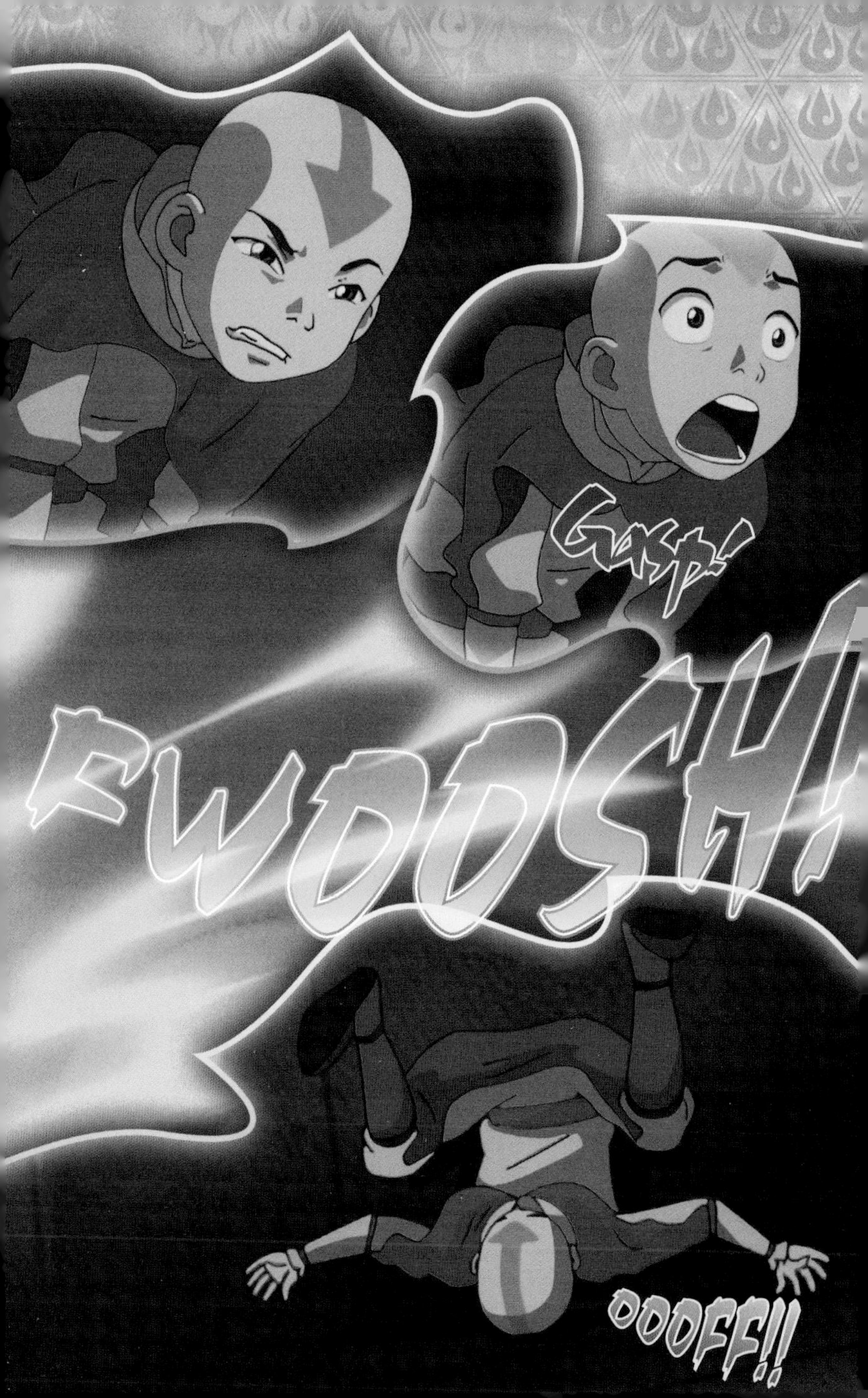
Gasp!
FWOOSH!
OOOFF!!

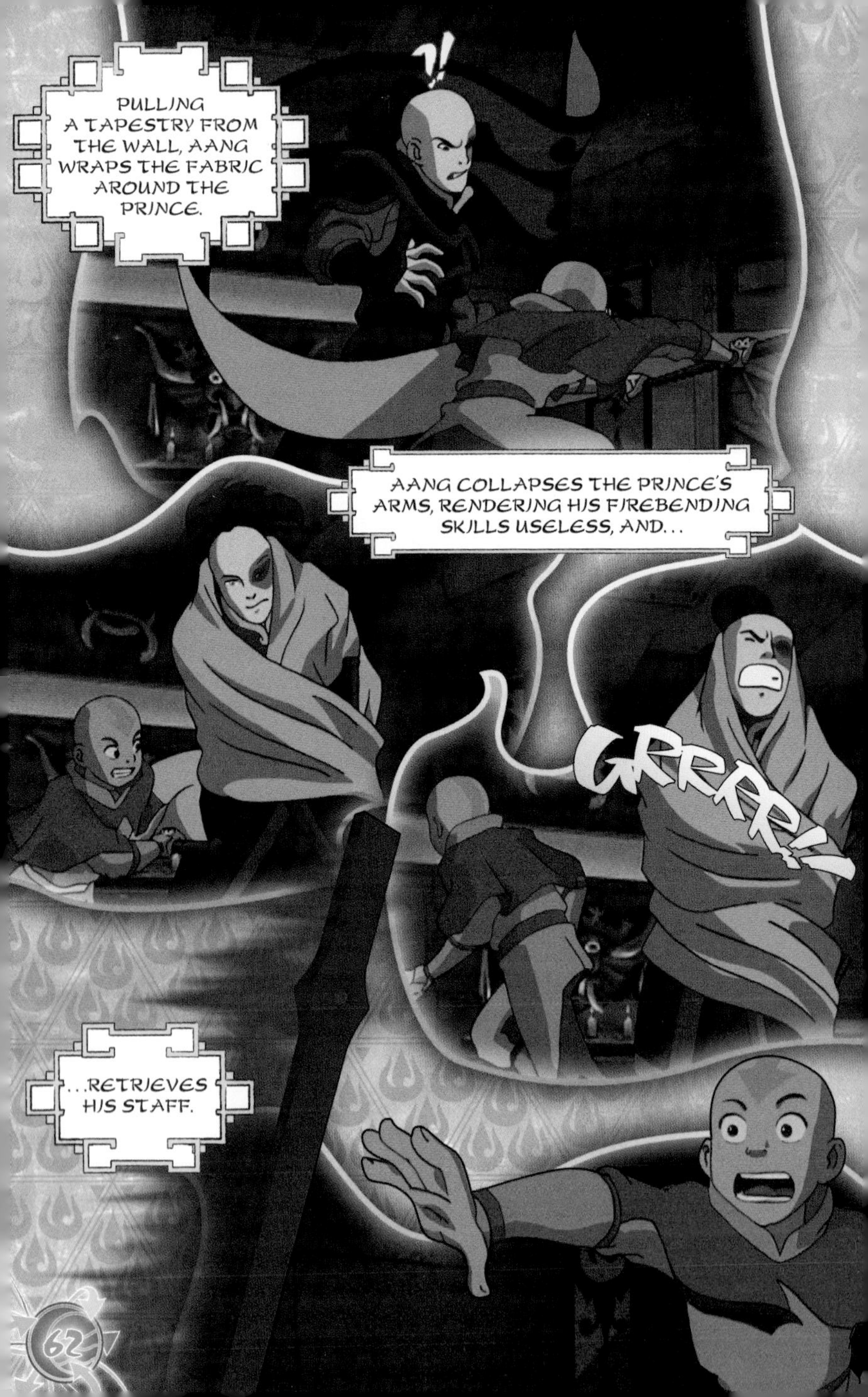
PULLING A TAPESTRY FROM THE WALL, AANG WRAPS THE FABRIC AROUND THE PRINCE.
?!
AANG COLLAPSES THE PRINCE'S ARMS, RENDERING HIS FIREBENDING SKILLS USELESS, AND...
GRRRR!!
...RETRIEVES HIS STAFF.

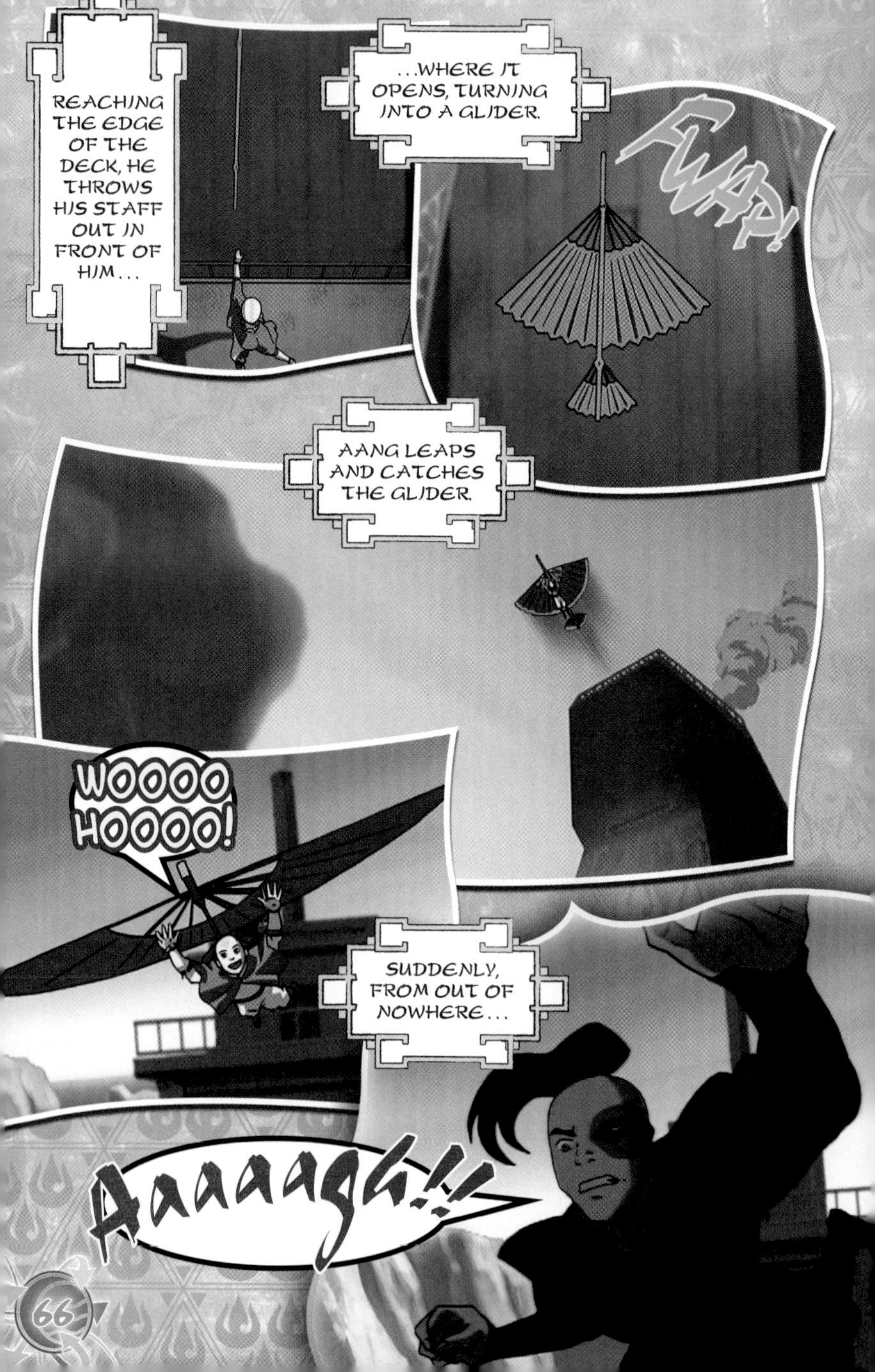
REACHING THE EDGE OF THE DECK, HE THROWS HIS STAFF OUT IN FRONT OF HIM . . .
. . . WHERE IT OPENS, TURNING INTO A GLIDER.
FWAP!
AANG LEAPS AND CATCHES THE GLIDER.
WOOOO HOOOO!
SUDDENLY, FROM OUT OF NOWHERE . . .
Aaaaagh!!

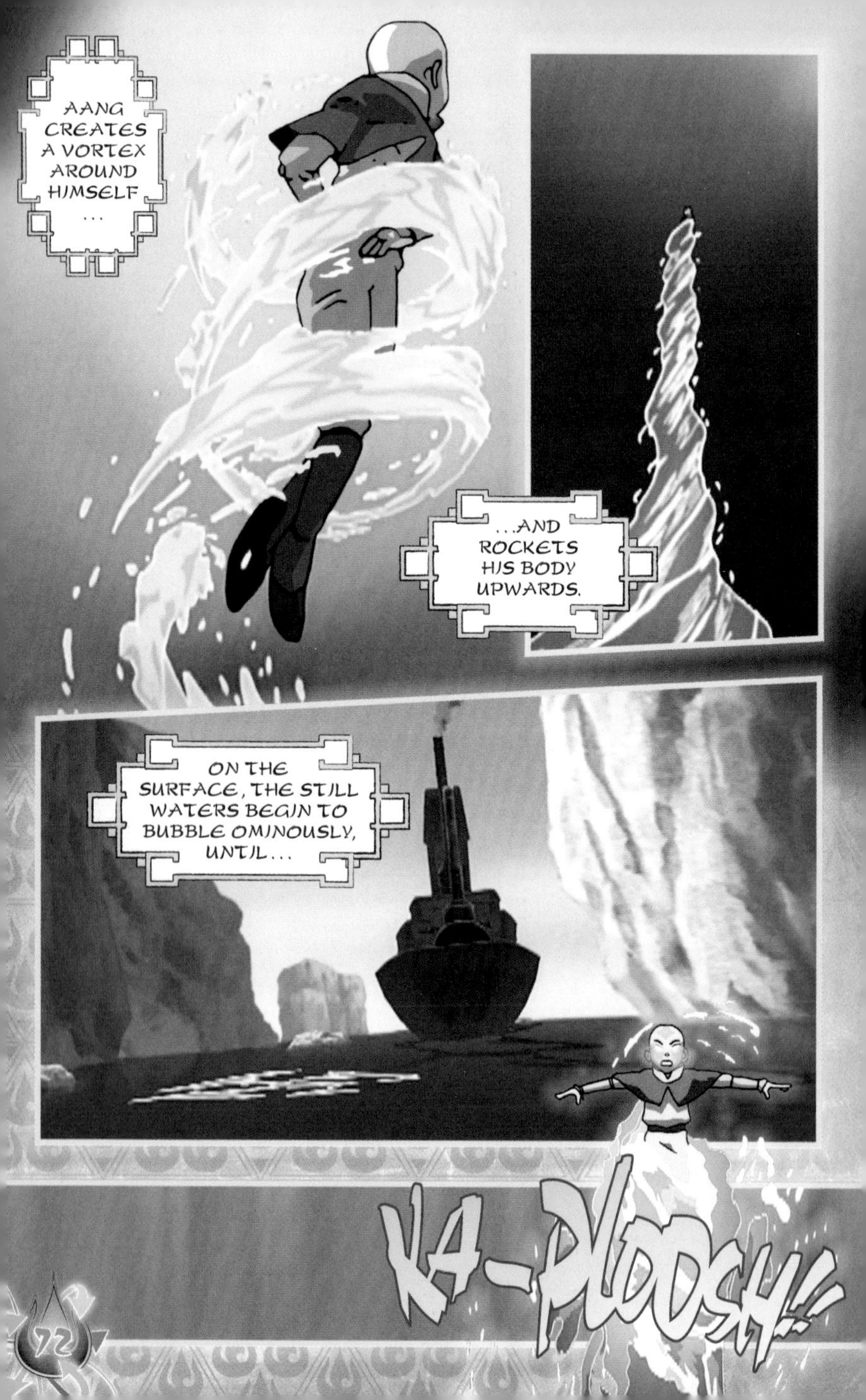
AANG CREATES A VORTEX AROUND HIMSELF ...
...AND ROCKETS HIS BODY UPWARDS.
ON THE SURFACE, THE STILL WATERS BEGIN TO BUBBLE OMINOUSLY, UNTIL...
KA-PLOOSH!!

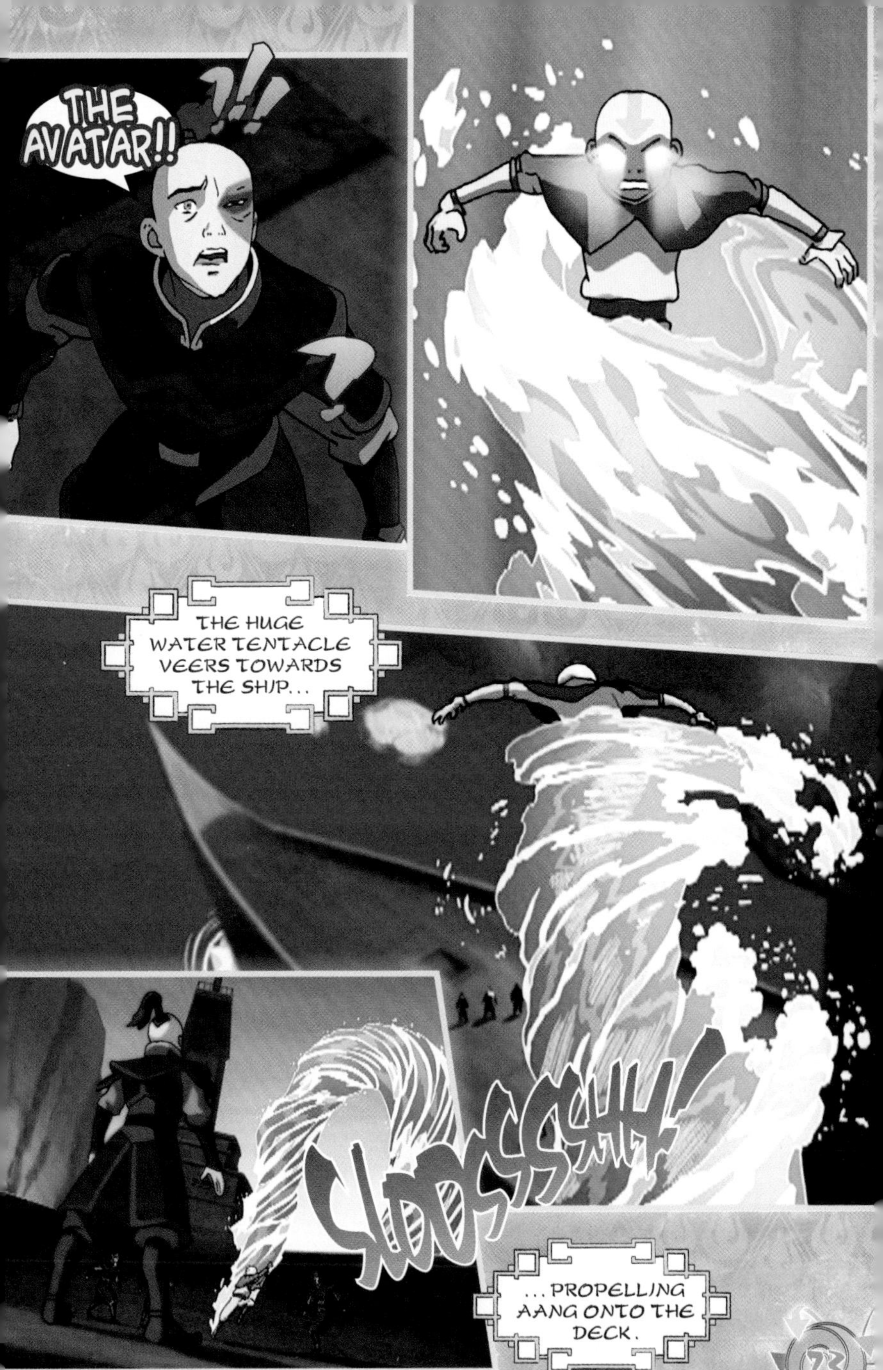
THE AVATAR!!
?!!
THE HUGE WATER TENTACLE VEERS TOWARDS THE SHIP...
WHOOSSHH!
...PROPELLING AANG ONTO THE DECK.

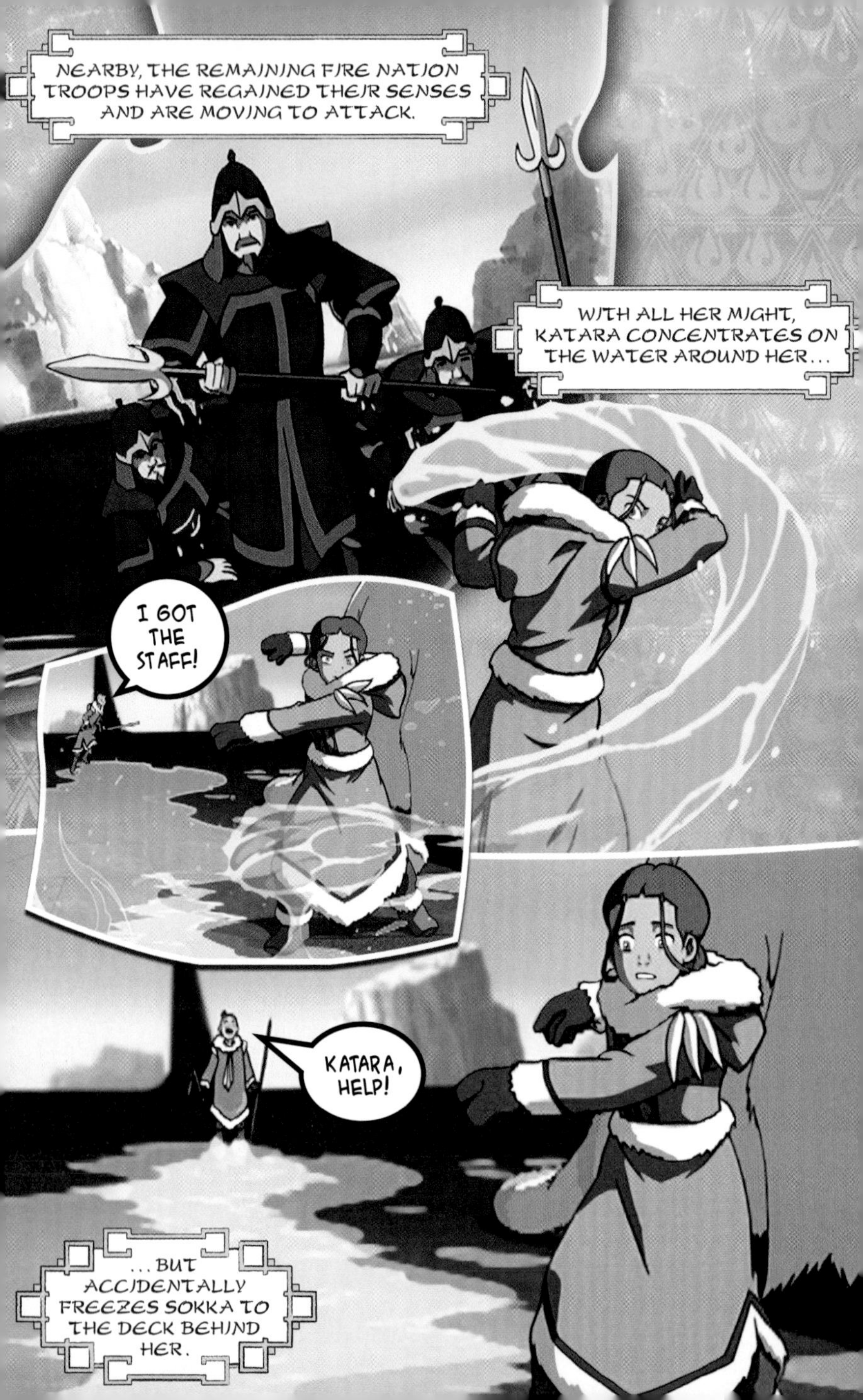
NEARBY, THE REMAINING FIRE NATION TROOPS HAVE REGAINED THEIR SENSES AND ARE MOVING TO ATTACK.
WITH ALL HER MIGHT, KATARA CONCENTRATES ON THE WATER AROUND HER...
I GOT THE STAFF!
KATARA, HELP!
...BUT ACCIDENTALLY FREEZES SOKKA TO THE DECK BEHIND HER.

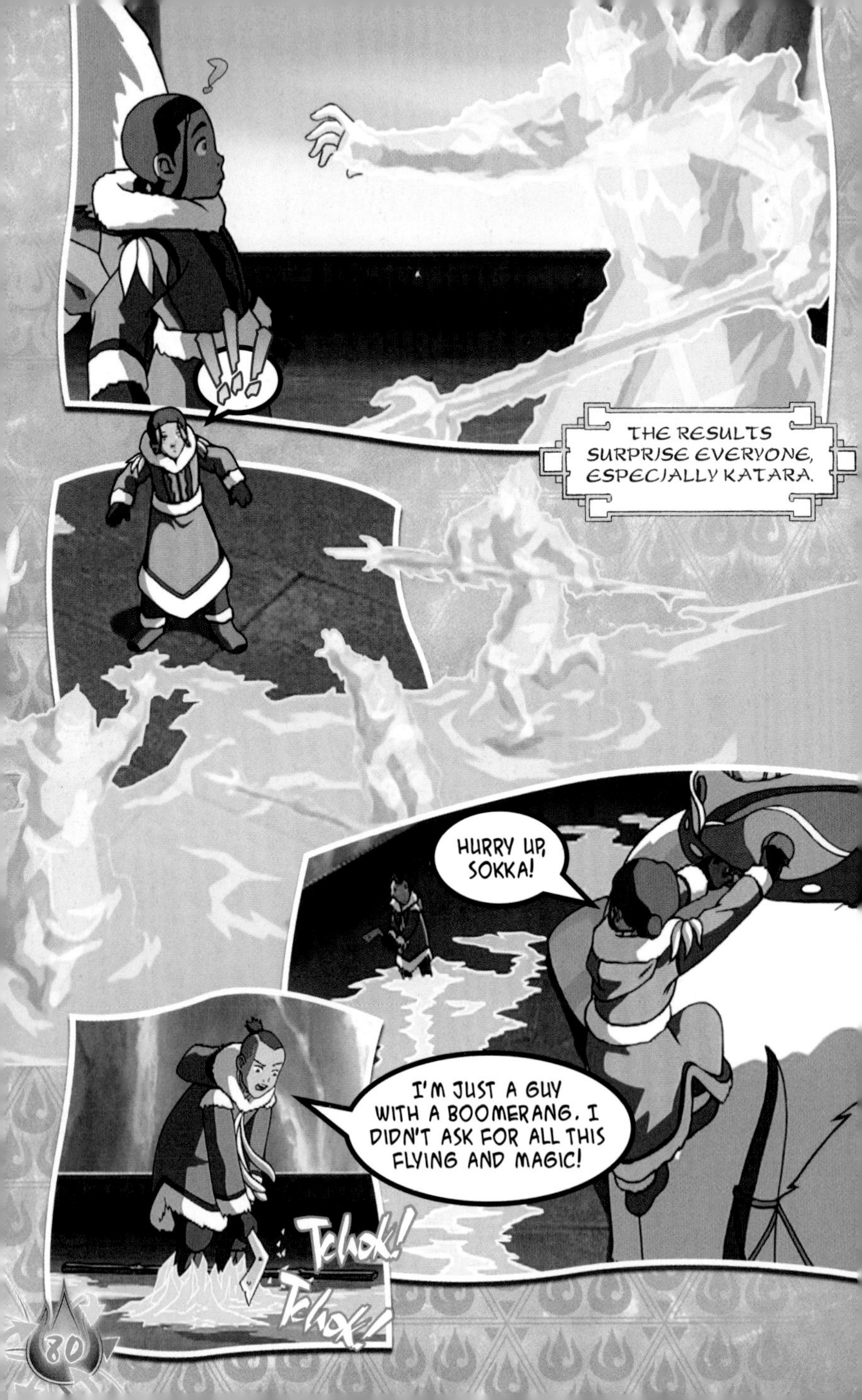

THE RESULTS SURPRISE EVERYONE, ESPECIALLY KATARA.
HURRY UP, SOKKA!
I'M JUST A GUY WITH A BOOMERANG. I DIDN'T ASK FOR ALL THIS FLYING AND MAGIC!
Tchok! Tchok!

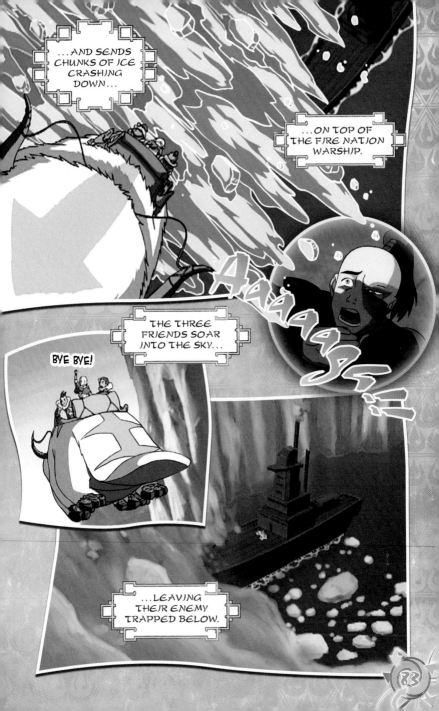

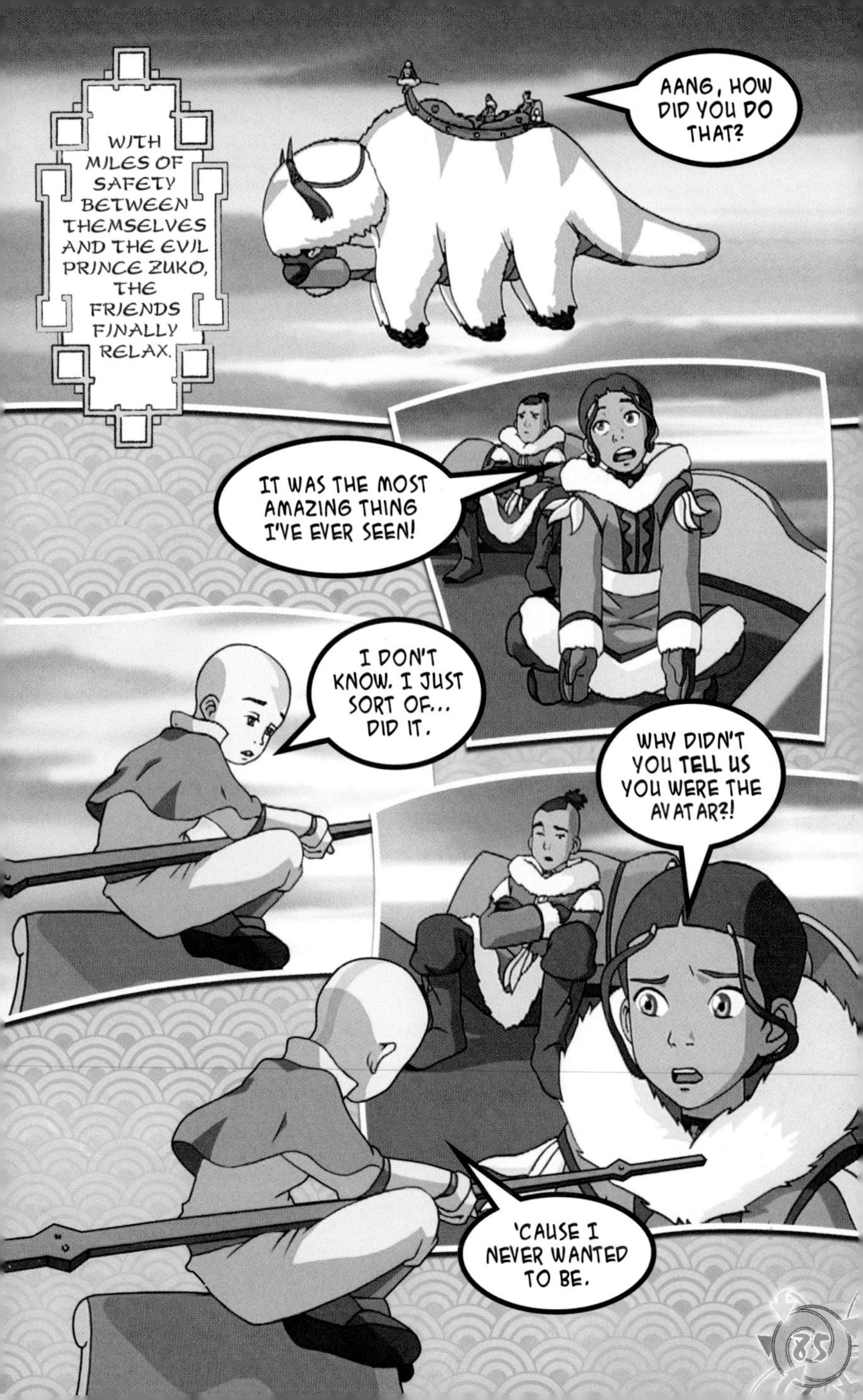
WITH MILES OF SAFETY BETWEEN THEMSELVES AND THE EVIL PRINCE ZUKO, THE FRIENDS FINALLY RELAX.
AANG, HOW DID YOU DO THAT?
IT WAS THE MOST AMAZING THING I'VE EVER SEEN!
I DON'T KNOW. I JUST SORT OF... DID IT.
WHY DIDN'T YOU TELL US YOU WERE THE AVATAR?!
'CAUSE I NEVER WANTED TO BE.

ANIMALS OF AVATAR

FLYING BISON

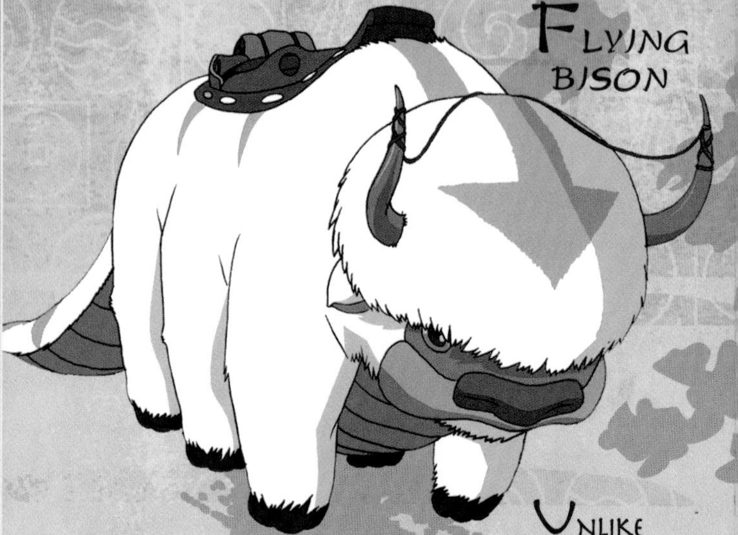

UNLIKE THE COMMON BISON, FLYING BISON ARE CONSIDERABLY LARGER WITH LIGHT TAN FUR AND DARK STRIPES ON THEIR BACKS AS WELL AS AN ARROW MARKING ON THEIR HEADS. THEY ALSO HAVE VERY BROAD TAILS WHICH THEY USE TO POWER AND STEER THEMSELVES IN THE WATER AND THE AIR. DUE TO THEIR ENORMOUS SIZE, THEY CANNOT FLY FOR LONG PERIODS OF TIME, OFTEN NEEDING TO STOP AND REST.

PENGUINS

FOUND IN ABUNDANCE ALL OVER THE NORTH AND SOUTH POLES, PENGUINS ARE DOCILE ANIMALS WITH AN INSATIABLE APPETITE FOR FISH, AND ALTHOUGH THEY HAVE TWO SETS OF WINGS THEY CANNOT FLY. SHY, YET FRIENDLY, THEY TEND TO AVOID CONTACT WITH HUMANS ALTHOUGH THEY HAVE BEEN KNOWN TO ALLOW PEOPLE TO USE THEM AS SLEDS FOR THE PRICE OF A FISH.

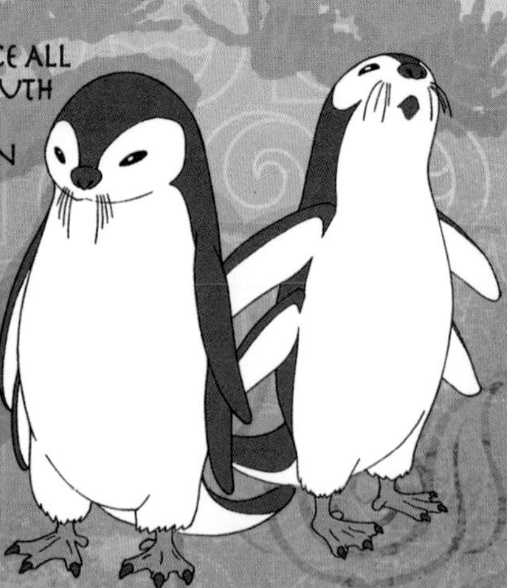

Winged Lemurs

Looking like a cross between a spotted bat and a black and white lemur, these creatures are extremely intelligent and have highly developed senses of hearing and smell. They can be trained, but if there is food nearby, they will eat it, even if they are told not to. Winged lemurs are nervous creatures; they panic easily and will screech in fear if they feel threatened.

Zebra Seals

Zebra seals get their name from the distinctive striping on their backs, which they use to camouflage their numbers from predators while swimming or hunting for fish. Zebra seals live together in small groups and avoid contact with other animals whenever possible.

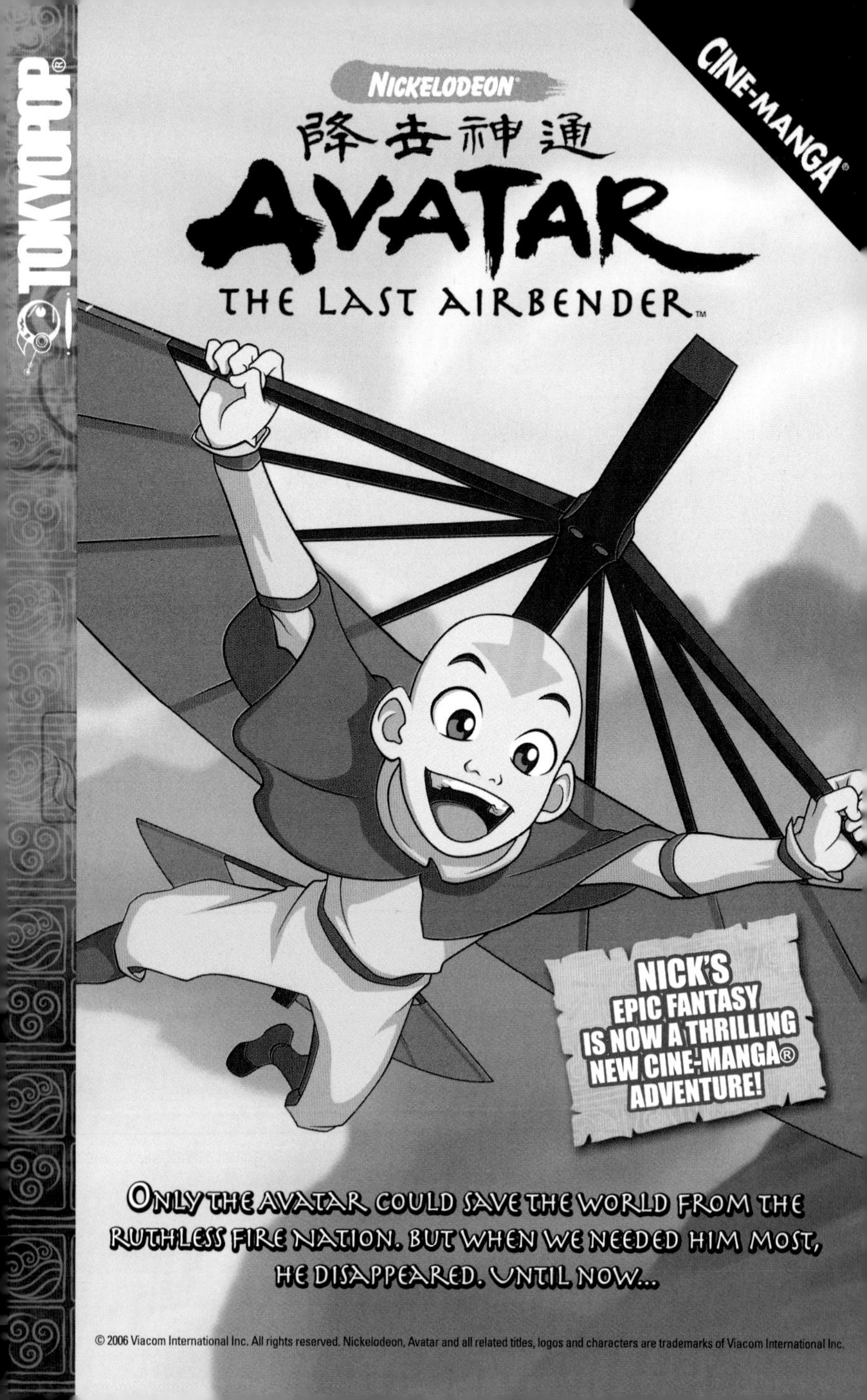
TOKYOPOP
CINE-MANGA
NICKELODEON
降去神通
AVATAR
THE LAST AIRBENDER
NICK'S EPIC FANTASY IS NOW A THRILLING NEW CINE-MANGA® ADVENTURE!
ONLY THE AVATAR COULD SAVE THE WORLD FROM THE RUTHLESS FIRE NATION. BUT WHEN WE NEEDED HIM MOST, HE DISAPPEARED. UNTIL NOW...
© 2006 Viacom International Inc. All rights reserved. Nickelodeon, Avatar and all related titles, logos and characters are trademarks of Viacom International Inc.

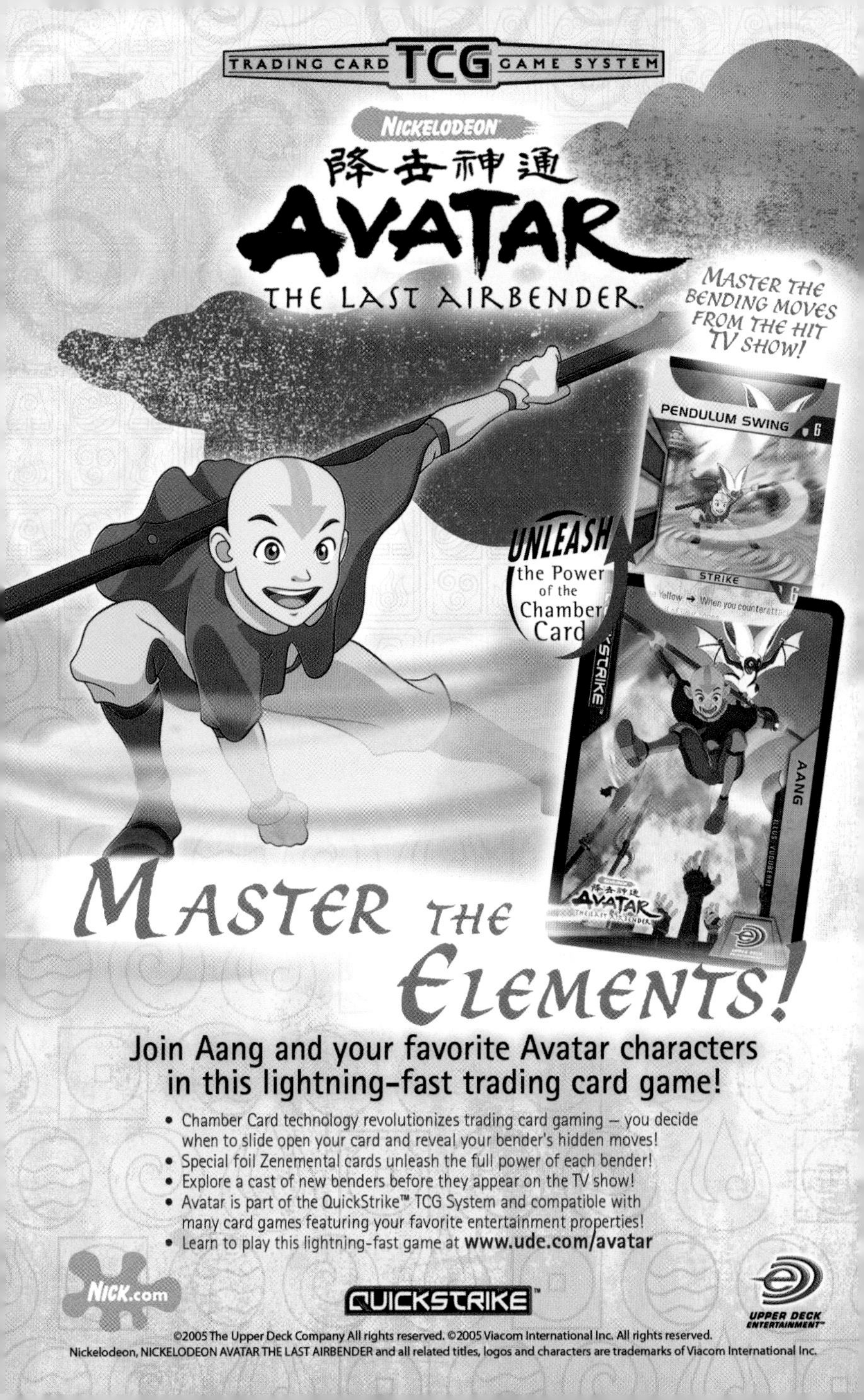
TRADING CARD TCG GAME SYSTEM
NICKELODEON
降去神通
AVATAR
THE LAST AIRBENDER
MASTER THE BENDING MOVES FROM THE HIT TV SHOW!
PENDULUM SWING
6
STRIKE
UNLEASH the Power of the Chamber Card
QUICKSTRIKE
AANG
MASTER THE ELEMENTS!
Join Aang and your favorite Avatar characters in this lightning-fast trading card game!
• Chamber Card technology revolutionizes trading card gaming – you decide when to slide open your card and reveal your bender's hidden moves!
• Special foil Zenemental cards unleash the full power of each bender!
• Explore a cast of new benders before they appear on the TV show!
• Avatar is part of the QuickStrike™ TCG System and compatible with many card games featuring your favorite entertainment properties!
• Learn to play this lightning-fast game at www.ude.com/avatar
NICK.com
QUICKSTRIKE™
UPPER DECK ENTERTAINMENT™
©2005 The Upper Deck Company All rights reserved. ©2005 Viacom International Inc. All rights reserved.
Nickelodeon, NICKELODEON AVATAR THE LAST AIRBENDER and all related titles, logos and characters are trademarks of Viacom International Inc.

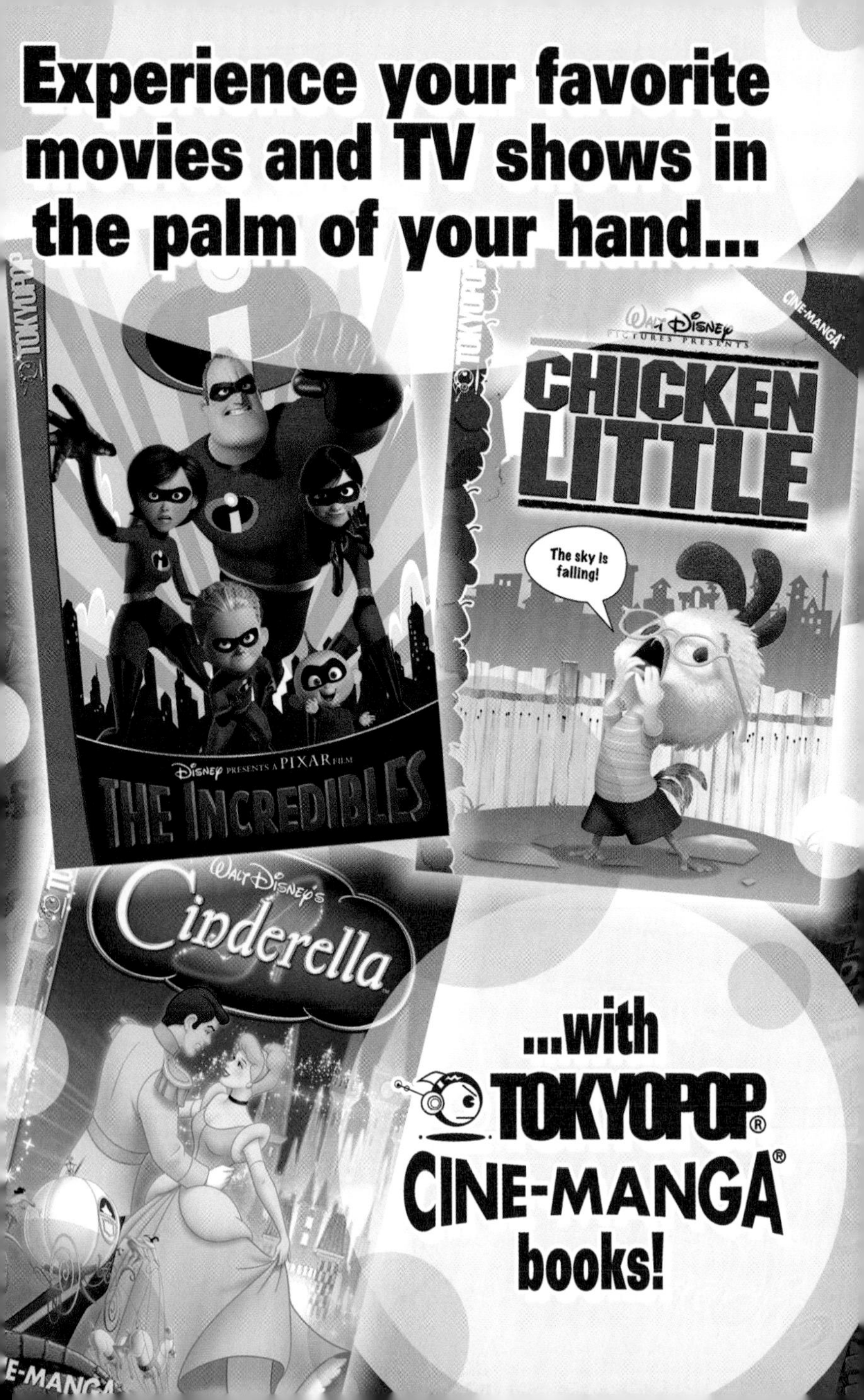
Experience your favorite movies and TV shows in the palm of your hand...
TOKYOPOP
CINE-MANGA
Walt Disney Pictures Presents
CHICKEN LITTLE
The sky is falling!
Disney presents a PIXAR film
THE INCREDIBLES
Walt Disney's
Cinderella
...with
TOKYOPOP®
CINE-MANGA®
books!